You, The Medium

Develop your psychic ability through home circles.
Raymond G Berube and Nancy Jane Isaacson

YOU, THE MEDIUM

First Printing, 1995
Second Edition, 2012
ISBN 0-9646600-1-6

Raymond G. Berube - Nancy Jane Isaacson

ACKNOWLEDGEMENT

We wish to thank all those who have given support and encouragement during the process of writing this book. In particular, thanks to the individuals who have participated in our home circles. Added appreciation to Lisa, Cathy, Richard, and Carol for volunteering to be interviewed in the final chapter. Our gratitude also goes to Bill Rowan for his permission to use the material delivered by Ramon, a highly developed Spirit channeled by Bill. Mr. Rowan has extended himself far beyond our expectations, and for that we are truly in his debt. This newly updated edition (2012) includes some limited new material added to the very popular first edition (1995), and corrections made to typographical and syntax errors discovered after the first edition printing.

Table of Content

Acknowledgement
Introduction
Chapters

!. What Is a Circle pg. 6

2. Nancy, On Starting a Circle pg. 13

3. A Childhood of Spiritualism pg. 22

4. Ray, My First Circle pg. 38

5. Ramon Speaks pg. 58

6. History of Spiritualism pg. 71

7. Interviews of Circle Participants pg. 81

Glossary pg. 109

About The Authors pg. 111

You, The Medium was written for those who believe that there is a life after death. That life may be called a "state of spirit", and we are able to communicate with those in spirit. Our point of view is that the reader is accepting of this philosophy. The material in this book teaches ways to communicate with those in spirit; an understanding of a belief system shared by millions throughout the world and one which has been historically proven to have been an integral part of many cultures throughout the ages. Home circles, a very personal and intimate method of creating the environment through which spirits can communicate. It is the focus of this book. Chapter One, written by Nancy Jane Isaacson, explains the elements of home circles. In Chapter Two she instructs the reader on how to start and run a home circle from beginning to end. Nancy then describes her early experiences as a child of two parents who were Spiritualists in chapter Three. Chapter Four relates Ray's introduction into Nancy's circles and how he found his "voice". He describes the initial channeling and subsequent data from the spirit of a historical figure who comes across the centuries to speak. Chapter Five is based on material given by "Ramon", a developed entity in spirit. This entity is channeled by Bill Rowan, a gifted medium from Australia through which Ramon has communicated for years. This information helped to define our concepts by explaining the purposes and goals which those in the spirit world hold for any on the world plane who perfect and expand their already-existing abilities to mediumship. In Chapter Six, Ray researches the history of Spiritualism. He presents historical/biblical evidence of the presence of spiritualistic philosophy and its impact on the present attitudes found in many current organized religions. The final chapter is a transcript of interviews conducted by Ray, with people who have sat in circles conducted by Nancy, describing how home circles have changed their lives in significant ways. After having read our book, we hope you will come away with a deeper appreciation of your own inner resources, your own uniqueness; your own wonder of the possibilities that really do exist when you allow your mediumship to develop.

CHAPTER ONE
What Is a Circle

I never met Allison until after she died. I met her when she came to me through a medium in a spiritualistic home circle, approximately two weeks after her death. The circle was held at Ray's house. The medium was another friend, Denise. Both knew nothing of Allison or of her dying. When the circle opened, Denise spoke first... "I have an Allison, can anyone place her?"

"Yes, yes," I said eagerly.

Allison, my children's cousin, had just died from a genetic disease. Cystic Fibrosis had taken her to Spirit a few days after her twenty-ninth birthday. When it happened, I wrote to her parents on a beautiful card with a solitary sunflower on it. The sunflower is the symbol of my religion, Spiritualism. My belief teaches how to communicate between the world of Spirit and the one in which we live. Little did I know when I wrote my card, how significant it would be in demonstrating life after death.

"Dear Gail and Bob," I wrote. "The sunflower always turns its face to the light- just as your Allison did. She's still the same sweet sunflower. She's just changed the soil in which she grows."

In a quiet voice Denise continued. "She has something obscuring her face. It could be a hood. I can't see what it is."

"I know," I said. "It's an oxygen mask. For some time before her passing she used a portable oxygen tank and was possibly in an oxygen tent when she died."

Denise continued. "Now I can see that she's dancing and is very happy. She's kicking up her feet and dancing around. She's telling me that HER FACE IS TO THE SUN. She's handing you a sunflower, Nancy.

I sat riveted to my chair, as these were almost the exact words I had written to her parents when I had sent THEM a sunflower.

"She's showing me some kind of clam or oyster shell. It's opening and she's pointing to the mother-of-pearl on the inside. I don't know why, maybe she had a barrette or something made of mother-of-pearl. There's some sort of significance to it."

"What color hair does she have?" I prodded, not wanting to let Allison go.

"Blonde," Denise replied.

"That's right," I confirmed. "How old is she?"

"She could be in her late teens or early twenties."

"I think her illness made her look younger," I explained. She was twenty-nine when she died and was showing herself to Denise as she had appeared when she was on the earth plane before illness. At the end her body had been ravaged from the effects of a long illness.

We thanked Allison for coming.

It took me almost an hour to reach my home after the circle. In spite of the time, I picked up the phone and called Gail, Allison's mother. Over a thousand miles away, she was asleep but quickly woke up when she recognized my voice.

"Oh did you talk to Hazel today?" she immediately asked.

Hazel was a mutual cousin who hoped along with the rest of the family that Allison would come to a circle and give evidence of her survival of the change called death.

"I called her today and told her I was going to call you and see if you had heard from Allison."

"I haven't talked to Hazel but told her I HAVE heard from Allison," I gently told her.

Gail cried as I related what had happened. Tears came to MY eyes as she put the pieces of Allison's message together for me.

"We were all with her when she died, her father, her sister, Sarah, and her best friend Amy, We kept telling her to look to the light. Allison loved to dance. It was her favorite thing to do. Just shortly after she died she gave her best friend, Amy, a necklace with mother-of-pearl on it."

Gail thanked me for waking her with Denise's poignant message

7

from Allison. I wrote it down before I went to bed. Several significant pieces were thrilling to me as a co-author of this book on home circles.

Allison told Denise she was facing the sun. As a medium Denise did not know about the significance of this statement. I had written that Allison had her face to the light (sun) on the sunflower card. Allison may have influenced me to write this. The sun had actually come out from behind the clouds at Allison's transition!

We, in our circle in Massachusetts, received verifiable information from a spirit who had died two weeks earlier in Iowa. We shared the joy of hearing from her and passing on her message to her family. Life goes on. We just change our location.

Denise, the medium, through whom Allison communicated, is an exquisitely sensitive person who developed her mediumship through **home circles.** *You* can do the same thing.

For generations Spiritualists and members of other beliefs have been gathering in homes and sitting in circles. The purposes vary from meditation groups to sewing circles to political action groups to book-study sessions. All gatherings have at least one common denominator – communication! The geometric form of a circle seems always to have been conducive to social intercourse whether it be at Stonehenge in England, Delphi in ancient Greece, or your own living room.

The Spiritualist home circle is a group of people, optimally numbering 3 to 10, whose goal is to develop their spirituality and mediumship. Spiritual development is the process of finding one's own path, upon which the soul travels, and then learning how to travel on this path to be eventually "at-one-moment" with Great Spirit (God). Infinite Intelligence is the goal.

Mediumship, a sacred trust, is learning to attune one's mind, body and spirit to another vibration (The Spirit World, The Other Side, Heaven, The Next Plane, Spirit, whatever you are comfortable in calling the place where people go when they die). Once attuned, the medium (using various methods) is able to communicate with friends, loved ones, guides, and teachers who are continuing on their paths, but in Spirit. The methods for development that the medium uses may include: healing, mental mediumship, and physical mediumship (trance, trumpet, transfiguration, and many others.

In this chapter we are going to discuss how to hold a home circle for the development of mental mediumship. It is my belief that many

psychic people do not have access to development classes or Spiritualist churches. I am writing in the hope that many will appreciate reading what has worked for me in the many years I have been holding circles in my home.

The Home Circle Or The Development Class

I believe the difference between the home circle and a development class is that in a development class one person serves as the teacher, prepares lessons and officiates in the development part of the class. The class may be part of a church's educational program or it may be part of a college or university. In a development class, knowledge comes from a teacher and her/his guides. In a circle, the flow of information comes from everyone. A development class is often the only form of learning available. Although I teach a development class, I do not think of it as the best setting for development. The development class, as opposed to the home circle, is a one-sided approach to teaching – one in which the *teacher's* opportunity to learn is limited.

In a home circle the focus is on the *group* and not on any one person dominating. If we imagine a campfire in the center of a circle with all the campers sitting around it, each camper is of an equal distance from the fire and is therefore receiving equal energy from it. Campers do not sit in rows around a fire. Those in the back would not get much heat, and those in front would get too much.

A true home circle is similar to the campfire circle; energy is not focused on one person or teacher. If that happened, the power of the group would become lop-sided and the circle would be out of balance. A circle can be enlarged by breaking it and increasing the distance from the center to allow more participants into it, but it should never be distorted by one or

9

more persons assuming power over the other members. People often give up their power when they attend a development class. They sometimes assume that the teacher knows more than the student, when often it the other way around. A good teacher draws out the knowledge from the other students, as she herself if also a student.

In a home circle learning is often indirect, with each member contributing as a teacher and each teacher, in turn, as a student. The power

is in the group, and the more unified the group is in their belief in Spirit, the more receptive each member will become and will therefore tap into the group's energy and each will become more sensitive and develop his/her mediumship.

Try to visualize a white light (God-Spirit) in the center of the circle and each member of the circle as being an equal distance from the center of that source. The energy flows from Spirit, in the center, to its members. It flows around the circle from person to person. When the energy is flowing correctly in a circle, everyone leaves it feeling wonderful.

Each member is unique and serves his special place in the circle. Some people will develop their para-sensory perception faster than others, but that does not mean that the other's potential is any less viable. I believe there is such a thing as a "born" medium and a spontaneously developing medium. I also believe anyone who wants to spend the time doing so can become one.

Each person has the responsibility to herself as an equal and important part of the energy and knowledge exchange. The learning that takes place in the home circle comes from each member, not just from the leader. The leader of the home circle views himself as a facilitator and an open channel for the sharing and learning of knowledge.

Actually sitting in a circle around a table helps to encourage the exchange of love, healing, and mental mediumship. Just as the act of eating dinner together as a family around a table promotes family bonding (with the meal becoming secondary to the togetherness) so do people who "sit" together for spiritual development form trusting relationships. The longer they "sit" together and the more their attendance is a circle, the more

bonding will take place.

Typically, circles will have people with varying degrees of their mediumship developed. Newcomers need to be assured that even though they may not seem to be developing yet they soon will, and by their positive thinking, will serve as energy sources for the group until they do.

The more trusting and open (lacking in negative thoughts) a newcomer is, the easier it will be for the group to receive messages for her from Spirit. This information will be a validation of the existence of Spirit (God, loved ones and guides still living after the change called death). It will also help the other developing mediums to learn to receive and give out

messages in a relaxed, protected and trusting environment.

A home circle starts when one person takes the initiative to start it. If this person is already developed and has been attending spiritual circles, it is easier to start with the format of the one already attended. This is what I did. I had been sitting for a period of seven years with other mediums in development classes. Those classes had been open only to members of the Spiritualist Church to which I belonged.

As my mediumship developed, I attracted many people to me who were members of other churches. They were interested in developing their para-sensory perception, but did not want to leave their own church to join another church and gain access to a development class. I remembered the home circles of my childhood. I was making good progress in my church development class, but I was afraid to start a circle--- afraid that if I did, I would be unable to "get" anything for anyone.

Spirit had plans for my "sliding" into the medium role. They sent me on a trip to Wyoming to visit my sister, Stephanie. As noted in Chapter Three (A Childhood of Spiritualism), it was there that I held my first home circle. Since then, dozens of people have come to my home to "sit".

During the last several years, one weekly group was composed of people from four states, another group met weekly with the same eight people for three years. Sometimes I have had two different groups a week meeting in my home.

My goals are always to have people develop, to take white light from

the circle and then, when ready, to have them start their own circles. Many circles are being held all over our beautiful planet Earth. I visualize overlapping Spiritual white lights covering this Earth some day. I see people sitting in circles at regular times during the week, raising spiritual vibrations, healing and growing. Hopefully people will come to this on their own, when they have reached that spot on their path that tells them that they are ready.

Two things I have never done: charge money for a home circle and tell people that they have to make a commitment in order to attend. I have found that those who really want to share and learn do not need to be told to do so. It costs me money to hold circles. I serve refreshments after the meeting. I believe it is worth it, however, as I do not have to leave my house to learn. My teachers come to me.

Also, I recently read in a newspaper a quote from an author whose name I cannot recall, but whose words ring true.

"Wealth is not how much money we have, but how much we have for which we do not take money".

I have nothing against taking money for mediumship and facilitating a circle, but at the present time I chose not to do so in my home, where friends and acquaintances gather for informal circles.

CHAPTER TWO
Nancy, On Starting a Circle

Here is how I hold a home circle: Pick a night. Invite twice as many people as you actually hope to have attend. Tell them there is no pressure to come, but if they can't, to please let you know as you will be starting the circle promptly and would appreciate not being interrupted by late arrivals. I always suggest that people arrive at up to one half hour early, if they want to make tea and socialize before the circle starts. Most people do this. Then they are ready to start promptly.

On the first night decide on the format of the circle and who is to be facilitator. The host or hostess who holds the circle is not necessarily the facilitator. It is probably better to have someone who has already started developing psychically to take this lead. You will understand why in a minute. The facilitator should be someone with confidence, someone who is willing to take risks.

The following is a suggested schedule for a home circle:

7:00 – 7:30

People arrive, socialize and get water, caffeine-free beverages or juice to drink during circle. Stress that no one should be under the influence of alcohol or drugs. Such substances bring the vibrations down even when the substance is a stimulant. It is also important to eat very lightly before "sitting". I encourage people to drink water during the circle. Water is a conduit for psychic communication.

7:30 – 8:00

People are in their places around a kitchen or dining room table, or perhaps sitting around in a living room. At this time para-sensory exercises are fun to warm up the people, especially if "sitting" is new to them. These exercises help demonstrate how we can connect with each other on the earth-plane via mental telepathy. Connecting with friends in spirit is the next step, and a similar one.

8:00 – 8:15

Relaxation exercises: neck and head rolls, breathing with diaphragm, silent meditation or guided meditation.

8:15 – 9:30

Circle begins: Facilitator says the following, or something similar:
"'We ask Infinite Intelligence that only the highest and best come to us and go from us". As we sit in this circle, we visualize two pieces of flint in the center. They are truck together and sparks fly out and grow into a beautiful white light that fills the circle, then the room. It encompasses us. We send the white light, our light that unites us, out into the atmosphere and around the Earth so that it may be seen and felt by all. We wish to attract spirits of the same vibrations.

Then, in the midst of the white light in our circle we see a beautiful green emerald. The emerald is the green of healing. We visualize it expanding until we are all inside. We feel ourselves whole, healthy and healed. Our circle in now a healing one. We place in the healing circle the names of any for whom we wish to ask healing. We start with our own name, for if we are healed, we can better heal others. Then we add the names of those we wish to heal. Pause as everyone says their names aloud or silently to themselves. Then the facilitator gives thanks, 'We thank Spirit for that which has been received.

"And now let us go around and ask for the help of our guides. You may do this in your mind or aloud. If you do not know your guide's names, greet them with their titles. For example, 'I welcome my Doctor/Teacher'. If you have loved ones in spirit, invite them to participate."

The communication part of the circle has several variations. Some circles begin with singing, others, chanting or drumming. It is fun to try different ways, but once the leader or facilitator notices that more messages come more quickly with one method, it's probably best to stick with that method.

Next, everyone helps to raise the vibrations by singing an up-beat song. The one I often use is *Zip A Dee Doo Dah*. While singing, I get in touch with spirit. Perhaps this happens because I am relaxed by it or of the energy generated by the group when it is singing in unison. Towards the end of the song, I will hear my first message. Maybe it will be a name, a word or a fact such as, "I'd like to go to the person in the room who had a hamburger for lunch, or corn-flakes for breakfast."

These "links" from Spirit place me with the person for whom I am receiving a message and when he or she answers me, their voice enables me to hear something more for them. This technique is called working with voice vibrations. For me, it is essential. I always get more information from people who validate what I report. The exchange of voice vibrations is significant. The more trusting they are the more I get. And the more accurate is that which I receive.

Other mediums do not work this way at all. They give out what they receive with no feedback or interaction. Some people are trained by practicing mediums to work one way or the other. I think we should work in a way our guides impress us.

There are two ways in which I conduct the message part of the circle. If the circle is composed of newcomers who are just starting to develop, we go clockwise around the circle. After I give the first message I pass to the person on my left. That person is encouraged to take a few moments, as long as she/he wishes to sit silently with everyone quiet, and listen to his guides or others who speak to him, show him a picture or symbol, or merely to impress a fact upon his consciousness. He has a right to his share of silent circle time in order to receive. Many beginners feel pressured and too quickly say. "I pass."

I close my eyes in order to better concentrate, when I am receiving a message. This is not always necessary when one's mediumship has developed, but in the beginning it is easier to "see" with one's eyes closed. I like to make my mind as blank as possible and instead of concentrating on receiving, I disassociate and forget the present. I tune out the others in the room and when I'm least expecting it, in this relaxed state, I hear a name or an image will "float" in front of my mind's eye, often for just a split second. This is the beginning of making a link between spirit and the person for whom I am getting the message. By verbalizing what I have received, I give the recipient the opportunity to acknowledge it, and then I usually get more.

During the second half of the message I often spontaneously give out information without consciously seeing or hearing it first. At these times I feel my guides, Dr. Thornton and White Lily are very much overshadowing and speaking through me. It is an amazing feeling and sometimes I am truly in awe of what I hear myself saying. Amazing as it is, para-sensory perception is a normal, but not yet fully developed ability. I hope that this book will help others to attain the psychic communication skills that are inherent within them.

If the novice medium receives something, he/she is encouraged to give it out no matter how trivial. What he receives may be very evidential to someone else. In the very act of giving something out, she may receive even more. It is important that the recipient of the message validate any message by acknowledging whether it is accurate or not. By using this method of taking turns, everyone gets a chance to speak and without pressure, they soon start participating.

If they do not receive anything, they simply say "I pass." At no time should anyone feel coerced into verbalizing anything. Even after giving a message, one concludes it by saying "I pass." Then, the next person knows it is his turn. A problem with this procedure is that it is difficult to receive a message while other messages are being verbalized.

When sitters are more developed, I resort to the voluntary, spontaneous-speaking-out system. In this method, whoever has a message starts then is followed by anyone who has another one. The only drawback is that assertive, well-developed mediums often overshadow beginners, who may be intimidated by them and not speak up. For this reason, it is advisable to make the group sensitive to not having anyone monopolize the message-delivery time.

A good way for a facilitator to get people started is to say something such as the following: "Pretend your telephone is ringing, you answer it and a voice says, 'Hello, this is….'" Have the group give the names that come to their minds after they hear "This is…" Someone may recognize one of the names given. If so, this is the beginning of a message. For example, once in a development class, we held a circle. A man who had not given out much, said he heard "Ken." I said that I knew a Ken in spirit and asked him what my relationship might be to that Ken? He said "Uncle." I said, "Correct." He then went on to accurately describe my uncle. Without being prompted by the telephone imagery, this sitter might not have been able to focus his clairaudience. It was his first message.

The same type of prompting helps developing clairvoyants. A facilitator might suggest visualizing a blackboard with a hand holding a chalk. The hand writes a name of someone in spirit. Or, the sitter waits for an elevator and when the door opens, a guide or relative of someone in circle steps out.

The use of this type of prompting is necessary only when sitters are new and have not learned exactly what to expect when Spirit conveys a message through them. Once this attunement takes place, it becomes automatic. But, like learning to play the piano before the keys are mastered, the tune does not always sound the same. It improves with practice.

When sitters really start to develop and have more confidence and want to progress, I encourage them to "do a solo." That means that for the first fifteen minutes or so of the circle, one person will give all the messages. The advantage here is that you don't have to worry if you are taking too much time. It's like having a one-party line (remember those?) as opposed to one with twelve. When you are doing a solo, all the messages that are coming in are from you. There is no interference and somehow it is easier to receive. It does take confidence to say, "I'll do it," but it is worth the growth you will attain.

When you start the circle, try both methods but work with one for a couple of weeks before you switch. Your guides are working on the spirit side of life to set up the chemistry for your special circle and the more constant the conditions, the easier is their job.

REMEMBER THAT NO ONE IS PERFECT NOR ARE ALL MESSAGES

Really good skiers learnt to fall safely so that they can sky on expert trails. Good mediums learn that not all the information they receive and give will be recognized. Accept that fact and go forward. Once I knew that it was okay for me to receive something that is not valid, my mediumship accelerated. I don't know why it happens. Perhaps the recipient has forgotten the information that you are getting or is nervous or fearful of acknowledging it. I too, once denied when receiving a message in front of one hundred people, the fact that I had lived next to a florist when I was in high school. After the demonstration I remembered that I had lived behind the florist for four years.

DURATION OF THE CIRCLE – WHEN TO END

During the first few years I held circles I started promptly at 7:30pm. The phone was unplugged, we did some para-sensory exercises, and the lights went out at eight. At times my neighbors saw sixteen cars in front of my house while it remained in total darkness for the evening. The circle lasted until I sensed the energy had dissipated. When I turned on the lights, without any clock except Spirit, it was always 9:30pm on the dot. The circle had lasted one and one half hours. I find that this is an average for most circles. If more people are attending, it will last longer in order for all attending to have some time. When there are four or five people, the circle will last about an hour.

I generally go around the table twice with everyone participating and then I announce that we are going to go around only one more time to see if anyone has any final message to give. I say a prayer thanking Spirit and our guides and ask that we walk a safe path home. We end the circle by singing softly "Good Night Spirit" (to the tune of "Good Night Ladies").

GUIDES-GUIDES-GUIDES-GUIDES

We would never be able to develop our para-sensory perception without those most important people, our spirit guides. We call them guides because of what they do. They guide us. They show us the way to develop spiritually and in every other way. We have attracted them. The more spiritual we are, the more spiritual the guides we attract.

I believe that we have two bands of guides, an inner band of five or six, and an outer band of a variable number. The outer band comes and goes as situations change in our lives and as our interests change. The inner band attaches to us at birth and stay with us for life. These guides come to

us for specific purposes. The roles they play in the inner band are the same

Raymond G. Berube - Nancy Jane Isaacson
for everyone.

Master Teacher

purple – white – gold

Doctor / Teacher	**Gatekeeper/Joy Guide**
blue, - sometimes two tones	leaf-green – yellow green

Protector/Healer	**Chemist**
red	some shade of blue (little green)

Healer

Could be medium to dark blue, possibly purple depending on the spiritual level of the healer

Above are the roles the guides of my inner-band play in my life. My teacher is Dr. Thornton. Many years ago I noticed that while sitting in circles or anywhere in the dark such as the sauna at the YWCA, I would suddenly have a neon-blue light flash in front of my eyes. I would then think of Dr. Thornton. In the summer of 1992, while listening to a lecture by Judith Davis at Camp Chesterfield, in Chesterfield, Indiana, she mentioned that when we see a "flash of blue light" it is often associated with the Doctor/Teacher. I smiled when I heard this, as my own feelings about the blue light that I had had for years were now confirmed.

Judith then explained the colors that she sees and associates with different guides in her band. I have incorporated what she saw, in the above chart.

In the course on Guides and Guidance that I took during the Seminary Week at Camp Chesterfield, Judith explained the roles of the guides. She used the analogy that we should think of our guides as staff members of our high school, a school in which we are the only student. Our Doctor/Teacher being the Principal and director of the rest of the staff. He is responsible for working with us on the life lessons that we choose. Our joy guide or Gatekeeper is like our homeroom teacher. We visit her at times of the day. My Joy Guide is while Lily. When I am holding a circle she is working hard to keep the vibrations high on the spirit side. She's the hostess

and she filters visitors from Spirit. Only those of the highest and best quality are allowed to visit and communicate. I have great trust and faith in her. Lily is helping me to develop my trance and trumpet mediumship, as well. Mental mediumship comes first.

Other teachers at my high school are my Proctor, Chief Rainmaker, who I see as my Phys. Ed. Teacher. He watches over me and is also a healer. The next teacher and member of my inner band is Dr. George Bradshaw, my Chemistry teacher. In the band, he serves as my chemist. He works with my physical body. During different types of mediumship, I believe that actual changes occur in the physical brain, enabling me to tune in better to Spirit. Overseeing those changes is one of Dr. Bradshaw's jobs. He has been working with me closely since childhood.

Master James, my master teacher, can be sometimes compared with the Reading specialist who visits many high schools to work with special students, a master teacher vibrates at a much higher rate than people on the Earth. He helps me and other to stay on a Spiritual path by making only occasional but special contact. I love my guides and feel the love they have for me. Once I was told of a guide who has been around me for a while, and who has joined my inner band. Her name is Sister Agnes. She is a healer. For the past several years I have been smelling the aroma of roses in the most unusual places. For example, I will walk into a room and be overwhelmed by the fragrance of these beautiful flowers when there are none present in the physical realm. These are from Sister Agnes so I can know that she is near.

When I returned from Chesterfield in October of 1992, I told people I had a new guide but did not mention her name. In January of 1993 at a circle in my home, an "Agnes" was brought to me! Several weeks later a new sitter attending a circle in New Hampshire brought an Agnes to me. The sitter was overshadowed as he said, "Your brother has a problem. I am a sister to him as I am to you. (In other words she is Sister Agnes to him and to me). Your brother needs you to listen to him and in that way you can help him most." Six days later in the middle of the Blizzard of "93", my brother called and said..., "Oh boy, do I have a problem!" I felt that Sister Agnes was perched on my shoulder as I listened.

The newly developing medium who brought me Sister Agnes was

new to pare-sensory perception, but had been meditating for twenty years. When he sat in the circle he felt comfortable enough to allow himself to go into a light trance so that my guide could peak through him. It was a very moving experience.

After many years of attending development classes, within the Spiritualist Church, I held my first home circle on June 24th, 1984. In the past, I've held one or two a week. People have heard about them by word of mouth. They call me, then they come. I have experienced great joy in continuing on my spiritual path by sharing and expanding my mediumship and in helping others to develop theirs. I have been attending home circles since I was a child, as a member of a family of Spiritualists.

CHAPTER THREE
A Childhood of Spiritualism

"There's no such thing as death!" my father often affirmed during his life. "It's just like changing your clothes," he would explain. "Our body dies, we take it off, and our spirit lives on in the Spirit World. The Spirit World is all around us, we just can't see it because it is vibrating at a different rate from us. While we are on Earth we have loved ones, teachers and guides in Spirit, who have chosen to help us, even though we may spend our lives unaware of them."

My father's guides were as real to me as persons that I could see. He talked about them and to them, frequently. He would see Teisha, his little Gypsy Joy Guide, in dreams. His Indian-Protector, White Horse, would make raps on the ceiling. Major Luftberry, his Doctor-Teacher, who was a pilot in World War I while on the Earth Plane, would speak to him and give him messages for others. Often, when Daddy would take a nap, we would hear him talking in his sleep. "He's just talking to Freddy," my mother would explain. I loved the story of Freddy.

SKEPTIC BECOMES BELIEVER

Around 1930 my father, who was at that time a skeptic and in his early twenties, visited California for the first tim with a friend. They were walking on a street in downtown Los Angeles when they saw a sign announcing that a famous medium, Arthur Ford, would be speaking that night and giving a demonstration of mediumship. Daddy and his friend were skeptical and devout Lutherans who, having nothing else to do, stepped into the hall looking for a laugh.

After his lecture, Arthur Ford started giving messages from "Spirit." There were several hundred people in the audience. My father froze when he heard Arthur say, "I would like to come to a young man in the back balcony, Leroy Isaacson." How could a total stranger know his name, my father asked himself, much less a name as uncommon as "Isaacson." He and his friend knew no one in the hall.

"There is a young man here from Spirit," continued Arthur. "His name is Freddy. He 'passed' by drowning, when he was 15. He says to tell you he is fine and there is no such thing as death."

Freddy, once my father's best friend, had indeed drowned 7 years earlier. Daddy was converted on the spot and went back to Illinois with the good news that Freddy was still alive in Spirit.

It was because of Freddy that my father, then my mother and grandparents, and almost all of my father's many Swedish relatives became Spiritualists. When I visited those relatives in the 1940's I remember that they had pictures on their bedside tables of their Spirit Guides. When they got together they spent evenings in the dark, sitting around in a circle giving messages to each other. As a small child, the laughter and the joy they shared produced a cozy feeling in me.

SPIRITUALISM: A RELIGION, A SCIENCE, A PHILOSOPHY

I have always felt that I was more fortunate than others that I was raised a spiritualist (believing in spirits) and a member of the Spiritualist Church and therefore also a Spiritualist with a capital "S". Many people do not know that since 1848 Spiritualism has been an organized religion registered as such in Washington D.C. Just as catholic with a "c" means universal and with a "C" means a church, the Roman Catholic Church. Spiritualism when capitalized refers to an organized religion with different sub-organizations worldwide.

It is a small church because its members do not proselytize. When people want to know more about it, we share our belief. We believe that all persons come to an understanding of a belief system that is true for them and we respect their right to find and develop what they need.

When I was young my mother told me that my brother and I were named in a ceremony at Camp Chesterfield, in Chesterfield, Indiana. When I was a baby a significant part of this ceremony was the sprinkling of rose petals over my head. I view this event as my initiation into a life-long

23

commitment to Spiritualism. I spent a lot of time in Chesterfield, the home of the Indiana State Spiritualist Association, until I was around five years old. We then moved away and for a long time I did not live near a Spiritualist church. My parents did not make a big deal about teaching us kids about Spiritualism; they just lived it.

Mother said that when Daddy told her about it, before they were married, she accepted it immediately because the philosophy was as comfortable as an old shoe and therefore very easy to slip into, comfortable because one has worn it many times and it conforms to one's foot. My parents also believed in the philosophy or reincarnation.

In 1952, while living in Connecticut, our family decided to move to Florida. Through a newspaper ad, they rented a house, sight unseen, in St. Petersburg. Soon after we arrived, we discovered that there was a Spiritualist church only two blocks away, the Church of Spiritual Philosophy. My parents joined that place of learning, and when they took their family of five children, soon to be six, they filled an entire row of seats. Mother and Daddy went to a development class one night a week. My siblings and I joined the Lyceum Sunday School. We often attended church on Thursdays as well as Sundays. My father was frequently soloist, singing songs such as his favorite "You'll Never Walk Alone", which implied that we are always in the company of Spirit.

All through high school I was in charge of the church library and the book table where I sold magazines and books. I sat in the foyer with my books and greeted people. Often they talked with me, then they went to a shelf on the back church-wall and wrote a billet.

The word "billet" means "note" in French. These notes were very special. Written to those who were dead, each was addressed to a guide or loved one in spirit. A question was asked then signed. The billet was folded in half and placed in a basket. I sat and watched the billet basket until church started, when someone such as my father would take the basket up front and put it on the table on the platform. The table was in plain sight of everyone.

Our church was usually full in those days. It had about 300 comfortable theater-type seats, on the platform were a piano, a lectern, a cross with "Peace and Health" on it, a table, a large floral arrangement, and two floor-sized candelabra each with seven candles.

The church service began with "healing", followed by a lecture, and ended with a communication service. There was much music in-between. For the healing service chairs were placed in front of the church. As soft music played, healers stood behind the chairs and people took turns sitting in them to receive healings. I always sat in the healing chairs when I was a teen, whether I was sick or not. The healer lightly touched my back, neck, head and shoulders. It was preventive therapy. I still do it. To me, healing does not necessarily mean being cured. It means changing one's state of mind, becoming relaxed and receiving strength and help from spirit *through* the healer.

It is a wonderful feeling to know that another person is publicly taking his or her time to focus prayers and positive vibrations on you. Powerful energy flows through the healer and into the person in the chair. Now some forty years later, I am a healer and often practice healing. I consider it a privilege to move my hands over the head and shoulders of the person before me. I keep my eyes closed and often see colors or hear messages as I heal. Sometimes people come to me after church and say that they feel wonderful and they too saw colors as they sat before me. I explain that I am but a channel for the healing force from Spirit. Healing is another form of mediumship. When I hear or see things for people while I am healing them, I share those things after the service.

The minster of my church in St. Petersburg was Rev. Malcolm McBride Panton. Slight of stature and of medium height, he had graying hair combed straight back over piercing black eyes. In 1952, when I first met him, he was 49 years old. He had left a more lucrative job as an advertising copy writer, to become a Spiritualist minster.

During the service, Rev. Panton went into and out of trance state twice. The first time was to give the lecture, the second, to give messages. During the lecture, a guide of his or another speaker from Spirit would use the minister's body as an instrument through which to speak. During the message service his guide, Pedro, would speak through him. On special occasions such as New Year's Eve, a spirit named Chicro would come through and forecast events for the coming year. These forecasts were always taped. Due to Rev. Panton's renown, the lecture was subsequently published on the front page of the National Spiritualist Association's monthly magazine every February.

For the communication part of the service, Rev. Panton would sit down at the card table on the platform, with the billets in front of him, and place a black blindfold over his eyes. He went into trance. He did this by relaxing and slumping forward until his head touched the table. Then, as he slowly drew his head up, his persona changed and his voice (still that of the physical body of Rev. Panton) spoke with the heavy Spanish accent of his guide, Pedro.

Pedro was very funny. He always joked and laughed as he picked up a billet from the pile that had been dumped in front of him by a platform worker. He would call the name of the person who had written the billet, the name to whom it was addressed, read the question, and answer it. Because of Pedro's wit, everyone enjoyed the message service, even if they did not get their own billet answered.

I consider Rev. Panton to be one of the greatest spiritual teachers I have had in my lifetime. Although we had two other teachers, Mrs. Heckman and Mrs. Belanche in the Lyceum, Rev. Panton also taught a part of the Lyceum. He taught us Spiritualist interpretations of the Bible. When teaching us a lesson about the Sermon on the Mount, he said that the First Beatitude, "Blessed are the poor in spirit" should read, "Blessed are the poor in *I* spirit: for theirs is the kingdom of heaven." He said the *I* spirit referred to the ego, and that those who were modest and not egotistical would get closer to God. He said not to call the ego bad, but that an overdeveloped sense of one could get in one's spiritual way and block the path. He taught us meditation techniques and, as children, he took us into the séance room. The word *Séance* comes from a French word meaning to *sit* or *meet*. At Rev. Panton's meetings, he shared with us his special communication skill, trumpet mediumship.

I have to admit that the first time I went into the séance room, it was scary. I was twelve or thirteen. My brother, David, was two years older. Peter was eleven, Karen was nine, and Stephanie, six. There were several

other children present along with Rev. Panton and our teacher, Mrs.

Heckman. Sitting around in dimly-lit home circles was one thing, but sitting in a black room completely void of natural light, was another. We trusted Rev. Panton, as he had been our teacher and minister for about a year, but it also helped that we knew that our carpenter father had built the séance room for Rev. Panton.

The special room had probably once been the living room of the parsonage. My father had removed the windows, filled them in with wood, installed an air conditioner and hung black velvet draperies over the one door in the room. The room had to be completely black so that no natural light would conflict with any light that appeared from Spirit.

In order for the trumpets to be used to magnify spirit voices, no natural light could be used in the room during séance. The reason was that a substance called ectoplasm was pulled from the medium's body and used to manufacture a voice box (or boxes) through which spirit voices spoke. They spoke into the trumpets and these megaphone-like instruments magnified the voices. Ectoplasm was also used to lift the trumpets and move them about the room, so that they could be better heard.

We sat in the folding-chairs that lined the walls. In the center of the room was a simple card table. On it were a Native American drum and three metal trumpets. The trumpets were about three feet long.[1]

DIRECT VOICE, A TRUMPET SÉANCE

Forty years have gone by since I first walked into Re. Panton's chair-lined séance room, along with my brothers and sisters, and other members of the Lyceum. I recall that I was very excited, somewhat scared, and yet open. I had heard about my parent's experiences and I had no reason to doubt anything that was to happen. Rev. Panton explained that he was going to turn off the lights with a switch behind his seat so he could go into trance, or a deep state of sleep. Voices would speak to us through the trumpets that were then on then table. We already knew about the ectoplasm. He said his guide, White Cloud, who was his Doctor-Teacher, would speak first then Maizie, his joy guide, also known as his gatekeeper, would come through. She would bring in all the other spirits who would

talk to us. We were encouraged to speak up when we were addressed.

YOU, THE MEDIUM

Rev. Panton asked us to sing "In The Garden," as he went into trance. Singing helped bring our vibrations up to that of those of spirit. The first sound I heard in that pitch-black room after we stopped singing was Rev. Panton's slow, rhythmical, deep breathing as he went into trance, was muffled by the faint, soft, slow beat of the tom-tom on the table. At first we didn't believe that we were hearing it. Then, it beat louder, and faster and faster until suddenly it stopped and a deep male voice boomed forth from the trumpet, announcing the presence of White Cloud! His voice came from the ceiling. He cheerfully greeted us, then introduced Maizie. She spoke in a soft playful manner, as many joy guides do. Her affect was in sharp contrast to White Cloud's and the other spirits of Native Americans that spoke.

One of the first persons she introduced was a man who said, "This is Andrew Jackson Davis, my children." We recognized him immediately as the founder of the Lyceum. We had read in our Spiritualist Lyceum Manuel that he had started it on January 25, 1863, in New York City.

We had studied how Andrew Jackson Davis, when depressed, had at times been visited by the spirit of Galen, the famous Greek physician. Galen had given him a spiritual cane upon which to lean. During subsequent depressions, Andrew had asked for the cane to be returned to him. He saw a flash of light and a transparent sheet upon which some words were written. During our séance (many years later), Andrew Jackson Davis spoke the words to us that had been given to him.

"Behold!
Here is thy Magic Staff.
Under All Circumstances Keep An Even Mind.
Take it. Try it. Walk with it.
Talk with it. Lean on it. Believe on it Forever."

The spiritual cane, his magic staff, was the ability to keep an even mind under any circumstance. I have always believed this staff to be a representation of Spiritualism.

Davis continued, "When you go out into life, remember that this is a special religion. It is not for all, for they are not ready for it. Therefore do

not tell everyone what you are going to learn today. It is for you." After he spoke, another calm, kind voice said, "This is Carl Johnson. I wish to speak to my grandchildren."

I spoke up without hesitation and said, "Hello Grandpa, I'm so glad to meet you." And I was. My mother's father had passed into spirit when my mother was only seven. He told us that he was around, loved us, and would be guiding us.

During the séance, each of us was introduced to and talked to two or three of our main guides. Many Spiritualists believe that each person has an inner band of five or six guides and an outer band of seven or more. The inner band stays with us for life. The outer band comes and goes as we need it. The guides are often known by different titles. For example one person may call his main guide his Doctor, while another may refer to this main guide as his Teacher. I believe that everyone has a Doctor or a Teacher, a Protector or Healer, a Chemist, a Joy Guide or a Gatekeeper, and a Master Teacher. There may be different combinations of these types of guides. Not all people have six in their inner band.

During this séance I met Dr. Thornton, who explained that he had been around me since birth and would guide me spiritually in my quest for knowledge. At that time he did not tell me much about himself. He was very well spoken, and used excellent English. Following him, White Lily and her sister Purple Lily, came in. These gentle spirits presented themselves as little Native American girls. White Lily was my guide and Purple Lily was my sister Karen's guide.

At some point during the séance as I listened to someone else's guide, I was startled and screamed when a hand grabbed my left ear and yanked it gently but firmly. All heard a loud laugh as an Indian announced himself as "Chief Rainmaker", my Hopi medicine man. He told me he pulled my ear to get my attention, probably using ectoplasm to form a hand to do so. Chief Rainmaker told me he would be around me for protection and for me to call on him when I felt the need.

At this point I think it is important to address an issue that many who are in Spiritualism, ask about. It has to do with what appears to be an extraordinary number of Native Americans who come as guides. "Why is it

always a Chief Something-or-other?" Ray, my co-author, asked that very question for months. We received our answer in the form of the same response from various people, some who were Native American, at Camp Chesterfield. The reason this happens is that we the living, are occupying the land that was once exclusive domain of these native peoples. They would naturally remain attached to their land, even in spirit, just as we will likely return, as spirits, to familiar territories and places. And they come as guides to those who lived where they once lived! People of other countries or continents would likely find that they would have guides who related to those countries. This is generally the case, but our other guides may well be from other countries or places. There is no hard and fast rule.

Before this trumpet séance was over, seven children had each spoken to two or three guides, in addition to Rev. Panton's own guides. The voices of the spirits had come from all over the room, above us, in front of us, behind us and beside us. Sometimes two or three people had talked together. We had been told that the trumpets would be moving in the dark. Occasionally we heard them bang into each other. At the end, White Cloud came back, thanked us, said "Good Bye", and trumpets came crashing to the floor at our feet. They fell from the ceiling, from whence the spirit voices had come.

The séance ended with our singing "In The Sweet Bye and Bye," while Rev. Panton came out of his trance. Lights were gradually turned on by a rheostat which allowed him to adjust the brightness of the room. We slowly left the peace of the séance room and returned to the vibration of our earthly life.

The first time I met my guides was when I was a teenager in Florida. The second time was the summer before I entered Smith College.

GUIDES, AGAIN

One weekend I drove with my future husband to visit my Aunt Milly, my father's closest sister, where she worked in Pennsylvania. As a hotel manager Milly had devoted her life to Spiritualism. She worked for many years as a hotel manager at Camp Chesterfield in Indiana and at Camp Silver Belle in Ephrata, Pennsylvania. She had no idea we were arriving that

weekend but was delighted to find us on her doorstep on a Sunday morning. When I asked about the possibility of a trumpet séance, she arranged a private one with a young medium named Roy Burkholder. Every winter Roy visited my church in Florida. I had seen him demonstrate his mediumship in church but had not had a trumpet séance with anyone but Rev. Panton.

For the first time I was alone in the séance room with the medium. I wasn't afraid, but a bit apprehensive. Any fear I had quickly left, when the first voice came through the trumpet. "This is Alma Morganthau," I heard with surprise. "I want to send a message to my granddaughter, Pam. Send her my love. On her desk is a doll that I bought her from Japan."

I was so surprised to hear from my best friend's grandmother, a woman whom I had met only once, that I could hardly talk to her. The doll, indeed, was on Pam's desk but I had not known it had come from Japan via Alma.

After Alma talked, my guides spoke. The very same guides that identified themselves through Rev. Panton, in Florida, now came through in Pennsylvania, via Roy. Again I spoke with Dr. Thornton, White Lily, and Chief Rainmaker. This time they had a fourth guide with them, Dr. Bradshaw.

"I shall work with you on the physical side of your development. Dr. Thornton will work with you spiritually and psychically ."

Years later I came to realize that Dr. Bradshaw occupies the position of Chemists in my band and especially in my brain, so that I can tune into Spirit and develop my mediumship. In addition to my guides, my grandfather John, and my uncle John, and Pam's grandmother, several other spirit friends and relatives came through.

After that séance in 1958, I spent the next eleven years privately practicing my religion. I did not live near a Spiritualist church again until 1969. By that time I had attended a college for one year, left, married (in 1959), and had two daughters, Lisa in 1960 and Sarah, in 1963. During those eleven years, I had felt the guidance of my band of spirit helpers but had often been frustrated because I wanted to practice and worship with other Spiritualists. I was also apprehensive of talking to non-Spiritualists

about my belief system. A few people in whom I had confided over the years had ridiculed me, so I had learned to remain silent.

RENEWAL

While living in Burlington, Vermont, I joined the Church of Spiritual Light and met Barbara and Allen Howard. She was a school teacher and a third generation Spiritualist and her husband, a locksmith and a wonderful trance medium. They devoted themselves to the church, but due to a lack of time, held no classes. During my six years in Vermont, I went back to college and was graduated from the University of Vermont, and started my teaching career with young children.

It was not until I moved back to Massachusetts with my family in August of 1975, that I truly began to develop my psychic abilities. The desire had always been there but the where-it-all had not. Over the next ten years I began sitting weekly in classes sponsored by the Spiritualist Church. I went back to meditating and most of all; I continued believing in my guides and Infinite Spirit.

In 1983 my mental mediumship began to mature. I was beginning to be able to give accurate information to my friends and in class. I was in awe of this ability but very happy with it. I began to tell my brothers and sisters all about it. They believed me.

In the summer of 1983 I went to visit my sister, Stephanie, in Wyoming. When I got off the plane, she announced that not only was she happy to see me but she knew all her friends would be too. In her little town of 6,000 it seemed that most of her friends were now into "New Age" philosophy, and she had promised that I would hold some home circles for them. In fact, she had one scheduled for the next night. "If I didn't mind." I groaned, but thought, "I guess it's time."

I made my psychic debut the next afternoon by giving a psychometry reading to a friend of Steph's. It was so accurate that I had the courage to proceed with the circle that night.

The following morning I was up early and took a walk downtown. It was before eight as I passed the local hardware store. The door opened and the proprietor, whom I had met only briefly the day before, stepped out.

"Good morning, Nancy," he said. "Say, I hear you got good stuff last night."

In a small town, word travels fast. In the end, I held five circles in the two weeks that I was there and gave several private reading – my first! I also came to the realization that either I was a medium or there was something transforming about the state of Wyoming.

My Wyoming visit was a transition time. I continued to attend church classes but was saddened by the fact that my church would not allow non-members to attend development classes. Many people wanted to develop their parasensory perception in a safe place, but were not yet ready to join a Spiritualist church to do so. They were not even ready to take a church-sponsored philosophy course.

OUR HOME CIRLCE

Before the next year was out I was holding circles regularly in my own home. At first I invited people I had met at a Unitarian Church conference. I attended the Psi Psymposium at the Unitarian Universalist Camp at Ferry Beach, Maine, 1983-87. This annual week-long conference was on spiritual development and included courses on healing, astrology, and reincarnation. Most of the people I met had spiritualist beliefs but had never heard of Spiritualism. They were "New Agers." These people came to my house for circles. Since then, dozens have come from all over the United States. One of these was my co-author, Ray Berube.

In the eighth year, Ray began attending my home circles. I had met him two years earlier while working as a Residential Counselor in a group home for people with mental illness. We both worked there part-time, while holding other jobs outside the agency. He developed rapidly once he made up his mind that becoming a medium was of major import.

Ray is a Pisces and I am a Leo, not a profound
match astrologically, but we soon discovered that our being born into the most creative signs of the Zodiac had made each of us a writer. We had another important element in common, too: each of us was born with a moon in Aquarius. Our personalities are similar and allow us to laugh at

things that no one sees as funny, to dress in either "cutting edge" clothing or in the oldest and most comfortable of things, and to love what many refer to as "The Occult". We are now working together to bring the "hidden" out into the open.

YOU, THE MEDIUM

Together we coined the term "para-sensory-perception". When I told Ray that I did not like the terms "ESP" or "extra sensory perception" because they implied that our sensory perceptions such as those involved in mediumship: clairvoyance, clairaudience, and clairsentience, were out of the realms of normalcy, Ray said, "Why not use 'para'? It's from Greek meaning 'beside", which seems to fit.

When I first met Ray, I sensed that he might hold a belief system similar to mine after he mentioned that he used to live in Phoenix, Arizona. Phoenix is not far from Sedona, a mecca of "New Agers". I think I broached the subject by asking if he had any interest in astrology. (I ask almost everyone this question, because often if they have a serious interest in the stars, they will also have interest in para-sensory perception.) He said he had "delved" into it some years earlier, but had not done anything with it since."

Two years went by, during which we became good friends. In June of 1992, I received an impression from Spirit to tell him that not only was I a Spiritualist but that I was also a mental medium. I invited him to attend a circle that I would be holding in my home on Sunday nights during the summer. I was not surprised when he readily accepted. It was time!

Ray came faithfully. For the first few weeks, he was not able to give out anything. He did receive many evidential messages from friends and relatives in spirit via the developing mediums in the group. After a couple of months, he gathered courage and began to give out information. What he thought were "random thoughts of his own imagination", when verbalized, became important messages for others.

Ray had a breakthrough. He learned a technique that worked well for him. It's an old one, one I told him about after learning of it during Seminary Week that August at Camp Chesterfield, Indiana. There, many talented mediums are blindfolded billet readers. They work much as my

teacher, Rev. Panton, did, but do not always go into trance.

BILLETS

When at Chesterfield, I wrote several billets at different services. Mine were answered among hundreds collected from the congregation during the church service. Blindfolded, most of the mediums would stack the billets, then hold or rub them against their "third eye" or solar plexus. They would discard billets until they came to one that felt right. They gave the exact name of the person to whom the billet was written, along with the name of the writer of the billet. All my questions were answered including the following.

I wrote:

"Dear Dr. Panton, what occupation am I best suited for? Love, Nancy."

The biller reader that night was Phyllis Harrison. She stood grandly on the platform, with her eyes covered, and her voice boomed out to the auditorium. As she stopped at my billet, she said, "I have a Dr. Thornton here who wants to come to Nancy."

"I'm right here," I responded from the third row. Phyllis, a medium who is also an astrologer, and is known for "telling it like it is", laughed and her deep voice boomed out. "Dr. Thornton says you know the answer to this question. You've already asked it twice before."

Chills went through me. He was right. I had asked a carefully crafted "test" question, but I did not get the answer I was expecting. I got a far better one. The two times before to which Dr. Thornton referred had occurred at Ferry Beach, Maine, at the Unitarian-Universalist Psymposium. Two different trance mediums had visited during the years that I had attended. Each had given demonstrations of billet reading. Each time, "coincidently," I had been chosen as one of 25 out of a group of about 100, to write a billet and have it answered. Each year, I wrote Dr. Thornton, "What occupation as I best suited for?"

The first year he answered through medium Carla Neff Gordan. "A medium, as this one is, only with your eyes open." (I would be a mental medium, unlike Carla who was in trance as a guide spoke to her and

answered billets.) Three years went by and Kay Mora, a trance medium from Oquossoc, Maine, voiced Dr. Thornton's response to the same question, only this time he said, "a medium, with four kinds of mediumship: healing, mental, trance, and trumpet."

When I wrote the question to Dr. Thornton at Chesterfield, he and I were the only ones to know that I had asked this question before. Phyllis, the medium there, related: "He says it will be three to six years until things really begin to happen. In the meantime, it doesn't do any good to know HOW to meditate, you have to do it!" Everyone laughed, even me, because I had not been keeping up with my meditation and knew what he said was true. I appreciated his reminder.

I have now returned to daily meditation, and so has Ray. I could hardly wait to try out the blindfold billet reading in the circle with Ray and everyone else when I got back from my trip. As I recall, I went first. I tape my eyelids closed with non-sticky surgical tape, then tied a scarf around them. This is done to create a very dark, intimate space called a cabinet. It makes it easier to concentrate. Before I did so, all the other sitters took pieces of paper (all the same size) and wrote billets. They addressed them to some loved one in spirit, using the person's full name and asked a question, then signed their own full name.

I bombed! I got nothing. This method was not for me. However, Ray tried it and he was very successful. He continues to get long, detailed messages with the blindfold on. He works well without it, but finds it easier with it on. This brings up the point that every form of mediumship does not work for every medium. With the help of our guides, we find out what works best for us. This is what this book is about, discovery of your own mediumship through the vehicle of a home circle.

Ingredients needed for your successful development include:

AN OPEN MIND - Maintain a positive attitude, surround yourself with it, and nothing negative can inhibit your development.

TRUST – in your guides. Affirm to yourself that they are there, even when you have yet to ascertain their identities. Address them by the roles they play in your band. Trust in your fellow circle attendees (sitters). Trust

YOURSELF.

COURAGE – to believe in what you are seeing, hearing, and sensing, and the courage to verbalize this information to others in your group. It's O.K. to make a mistake. Telephone lines break down on the earth plane and when they do, we just wait a little while until communication is re-established, then dial again.

HEALING – having a healing feeling about yourself will help you keep well and project the same glow to others. In your mind surround yourself with white light for Spirit and green or blue light for healing. Know you are protected. "If Spirit is with you, who can be against you!" Spirit is the white spark within us all. Healing fans this small flame and makes it grow and illuminate us, transforming us into healthy people.

PATIENCE – it can take months, even years, to develop para-sensory perception and a lifetime to refine it.

FAITH – that you too can become a medium to channel your para-sensory perception and to guide others.

Take all these ingredients and hold them in your heart, and grow. Your growth can be an on-going experience shared by members of the circle. From these experiences relationships develop. Bondings occur that may become life-long associations, friendships, and sometimes even marriages.

After an intimate experience in a circle where messages have been received from loved ones, a closer feeling is created between oneself, other members, and Spirit. This is truly where development takes place. People just plain "FEEL GOOD" at the end of a circle. They have shared in other people's most precious and intimate moments. The process of giving messages and receiving them is so fulfilling emotionally and spiritually that one can not help but feel the closeness of those in spirit and those on the earth plane. The act of sitting in a darkened room, in a circle, with others who have a similar purpose creates great energy, and camaraderie. This exchange between people operates on a higher level because money is not the object. Love is!

CHAPTER FOUR
Ray, My First Circle

The Beginning

Lights are lowered. The room is in near-darkness. Everyone is seated comfortably in separate chairs that form a circle, each simultaneously in a group yet separate. Relaxation of the body helps set a tone of quietude.

Imaging unites the minds. We put forth the white light formed within the circle's center, projecting it to the universe and to loved ones and known ones who need healing. Names are called out quietly, directed to the center, as these participants unite to form a common experience. The uniting effort helps prepare the sitters' minds to be responsive to Spirit; calling to welcome spirits who will, hopefully, manifest themselves.

A quiet moment. Mind-sounds and visions come and go. Thoughts, impressions are allowed to be, all the while awaiting something like a word within, a whisper or fleeting image or visage standing out among the many, as one of significance. Around me they begin to voice things heard and seen. Not always as an internal image, a mind's thought, but sometimes somewhat solid a few feet away, standing behind or beside, and present within the room; something which may or may not be acknowledged.

There's a Frank..., a short man with a mustache...,wire-rimmed glasses...,wearing a leather apron and holding an arm-load of food..., coming to offer it." One of the people present speaks of what is seen or felt as an impression.

"I think I know him," another responds. She bids him welcome. "Can you go with this a bit further...?"

Recognized, indentified by certain body characteristics or specific structures of the room in which he is seen, his manner and speech, he is claimed as the man who owned the shoe-repair shop beneath her tenement when she was a child. He provided food and clothing in those times when her father had been incapacitated by illness and unable to work, and mother functioned poorly due to depression. He had shown kindness and concern for her and her brothers and sisters at a time when it seemed no one else cared and the desperateness she had felt was, for a time, relieved. Once again, he has brought her assurance and comfort, hope. The evidential content of the message leaves no doubt the spirit is who he is thought to be.

Two more similar occurrences, each containing the kind of detail only known from absolute personal knowledge, made it evident that they were not the kind of "messages" I had seen at fairs and with card-readers, where what had been said was so vague or general that anyone wanting to hear a message, could identify and claim it. It was not the case, that night. The contacts were filled with concrete, evidential material.

This was how my first meeting went, as a new member of a circle that had been meeting for some years. I had been unable to focus on my own thoughts, fascinated by some rapid-fire information, information delivered by several members obviously well developed in mediumship. In spite of how unusual or extraordinary this may seem to most who might have witnessed the evening, none of those present save myself, seemed distracted: all appeared to take the course of the evening with stride, as though the events were routine and without sensation.

And for some, speaking to spirits and receiving impressions from them seems no more unusual than it does for others to have dialogues with heaven through prayer or contemplation, or praying to saints or gods and believing that these prayers will be answered. The naturalness with which these circle participants went into our meetings, made the events seem less extraordinary and easier to accept.

Developing Self-Trust

It took several meetings before I could overcome my anxiety about speaking what I believed were random thoughts and imaginings, fleeting segments which, I was convinced, were constructions of my own fertile imagination! Being a writer, I understood how, allowed free reign, my mind

could on its own initiative provide all the material for a book with
little effort on my part, to construct! So it was with apprehension that I
voiced my doubts of whether I was hearing my creativity and rambling
brain, or whether I was actually receiving material from spirits who had
accompanied us. Reassurances from Nancy and several others gave me
courage to venture some response after the fourth or fifth meeting. To my
surprise, the information I gave out was acknowledged.

I remember asking the same question repeatedly the first few weeks,
and getting the same response from Nancy and Stanley, another member of
the circle.

"What am I looking for, how do I know when I'm receiving
something?" So many times in those first meetings, I had waited quietly,
listening to those around me giving out information in a sometime-rapid
fashion, my mind dancing with thoughts, images, wisps and fleeting
fragments of ideas, all coming and going and my concentration distracted,
trying to brush all this away to allow those hoped-for messages to get
through. They urged me to trust my instinct and ear
(inner-ear); take a leap of faith by voicing what was going through my mind.
To my surprise, the impressions I saw and heard within my thoughts were
usually claimed and identified by the person to whom I said it was directed.
Of course there were times when what I gave out, had no meaning to
anyone. But this happened fairly frequently to many of the other circle
participants too, some who were well developed and tuned into their ability.
I came to learn to trust my intuition and be less concerned with whether I
would be correct. Being wrong with information, describing someone who
no one claims, giving details that are not confirmed or recognized, all these
things are a normal part of a circle session where people are developing.

Fine-Tuning The Mind

Being able to perceive spirit messages has much to do with fine-
tuning the mind in order to focus on emptiness, allowing impressions to get
through, uncluttered with personal "mind-stuff". Like meditation, which
trains the mind to go inward an focus there, or in some forms, achieving the

absence of focus or direction, acting as a channel for spirit messages is sharpened by practice and the exercise of meditation.

Just as living people make mistakes in hearing messages, or make errors of clarity in transmitting information, so too do those in spirit. Someone having recently gone into spirit is much less able to communicate effectively, exercising those facilities needed, and more likely to be confused or still unnerved by the experience of having gone into spirit (died).

Fear, preoccupation with worldly problems, distrust or serious skepticism, emotional imbalance or disturbance, all these things can seriously influence how effectively one may be able to participate. These elements also have serious impact on the productivity and receptivity of the group. Negative vibrations and feelings can be perceived by the more sensitive members of the group who can be thrown off by having the circle's energy disrupted.

Many factors may contribute to inaccuracy. Attention is put on trying to give out what is sensed, and additional information helps increase the veracity of impressions, leading to a more solid connection with those spirits present. It is a matter of attunement!

Reason and Purpose of Participation

Why would anyone want to join a circle? There are as many answers as there are people who have participated. My own was two-fold. Having always had interest in elements of spiritualism without actually practicing it in any organized way, and having had a long-standing curiosity about things paranormal, I havehad an open mind about events which defy description or explanation in the normal sense. It is this curiosity that led me to be part of the group that witnessed psychic surgery in Phoenix, Arizona some years ago.

How easy it is for those of us who hear reports of these strange events, to dismiss them as the result of hallucinatory behavior, vivid and active imaginations, individual or mass hallucinations or hysterics and so on! Since that psychic healing experience, I understand the meaning behind the statement "I know what I saw!"

YOU, THE MEDIUM

Having studied and used hypnosis in private practice, I was aware and looked for any signs of individual or mass induction by the two men who performed the surgery. None was detected, and slight of hand was impossible, as their hands were *always* visible and observed by others. This is just another example of various phenomena that have remained unexplained or for which there are no rational or "scientific" explanations. The well-known TV personality and magician "Randy" claims to have "exposed" many of these phenomena but for my own thinking, some of his disclosures are nothing more than conjured demonstrations that seriously do not eliminate the existence of the "supernatural", and are as questionable as what he seeks to discount. Some things simply **are**!

My second purpose for joining Nancy's circles was to get back to stimulating that part of the brain that has to do with intuition and creativity. I had given up meditation, not with intent, but more so with having new demands put on my time (a poor excuse now recognized). I had experienced a long and dry period in my writing. When Nancy asked whether I would be interested in joining her weekly group, I recognized the opportunity to re-institute a way of life I had neglected. The hoped-for return of creativity and spark that had much to do with things esoteric, had been recovered.

There are many reasons for joining a circle. To those who, like myself, were raised Roman Catholic or of some other faith that discourages or prohibits the participation or belief in spiritualistic activities, reflection should demonstrate no conflict between the two. Although the structure of church and rituals are different, the belief in after-life, spirits, and god pose no conflict. Any enmity that exists is the result of some notoriety at the turn of the 20th century when Spiritualism became overwhelmingly popular. Many religious organizations perceived this enthusiasm as a threat to their own authority. Many who believe in spiritualism continue to be faithful to their own religious affiliations.

My own curiosity was stirred once I had attended several of Nancy's circles. I heard for myself the kind of identifiable and evidential messages given to others who were pleased for the helpful assistance often incorporated in their communications. I have been the recipient of

messages which have startled and amazed me for their accuracy and specific details. The following is an example.

At one of my first circles, someone stated that he had received the impression that I would soon sell something I had written, and that would be the result of my having answered an ad in a trade journal or magazine. At the time, I bought none of these publications, having dropped my subscription to
WRITERS DIGEST well over a year before. I thought this message unlikely. Two days after, I received a subscription offer from WRITERS DIGEST, urging me to "come back". Picking up on the coincidence, I sent my subscription. Within three weeks, the first issue arrived and in it were three ads from agents looking for new writers. I sent off manuscripts and of those three, two requested additional material for possible representation. The sale is just down the road! (As of the current update to this edition, no sales took place as a result of the incident just related).

These kinds of anecdotes abound and some are related in chapter seven as interviews and personal experiences, to illustrate the wide range of benefits and aid that can be obtained from receiving messages from spirits.

As a writer and amateur historian, I looked forward to the possibility of being able to get communication from several historical personalities, it has been done before in whom I have had a long-time interest. But because of the span of centuries I was not sure if the personalities could connect. When I posed this question to Nancy and a circle participant, they suggested it would be highly unlikely because the personalities might have become diluted through the centuries and multiple reincarnations. Each time we met during the interim periods, I sent out hope and a sincerer wish for one personality in particular, to come through. Should this be possible, I would benefit from the additional and more personal insight of the period and issues of which I have written in a published novel, Antinoos and Hadrian, also available on Amazon.

A Voice From The Past

It has been several weeks since the above paragraph was written. Each week, I hoped something would come through and that a connection

would be made with the historical individual from whom I was hoping. I had no idea that the connection would occur so soon or that it would be as startling and evidential as it turned out to be. As exampled by interviews reported in chapter seven, many who practice spiritualism experience one particular event that, because of the individual material involved and disclosed, becomes the pivotal element that solidly legitimizes Spiritualism. My own pivotal event is related here as I recorded the experience shortly after the session. The person who channeled through is/was an intimate of the Emperor Hadrian, ruler of the Roman Empire during part of the second century. Antinoos was deeply influential in Hadrian's life, and Roman history might read differently without him.

Cathy sits beside me. She calls my name and asks whether I recognize anyone named Anthony. He is male. Having a name in mind, I ask if she has the name right, if it could be Anti...., and she responds "Antonette?", but that the spirit is male.

"It's the cover...., he says you must change the cover design...., the cover needs to be changed," she continues relating what she hears the spirit saying.

Cathy knows nothing about me being a writer, and certainly knows nothing about my having written a novel about Antinoos, the close companion of the Emperor Hadrian. I have been sending out the thought that I have wished to hear from Antinoos, if possible, for the past two months. In each circle I attend, when the relaxation exercise is performed at the beginning to set up a state of calm and inward focusing I have put out the hope that Antinoos could communicate with me. Even during my working day the thought has been with me and I have sent it out. But my expectations were not high primarily due to the length of time separating his period in history from my own. So many other lives in his reincarnations may have diluted the essence he

held in the second century. I was warned by both Nancy and Stanley that going back that far was unlikely. But here he was!

I ask Cathy if she can get deeper into him, if she can answer a question that will be answered with a yes or no.

"Is the way I wrote the ending correct?" I ask.

Cathy quickly answers "no", and Abdo, another circle member sitting across the room says, "definitely no!", confirming Cathy's message from Antinoos, and corroborating the absoluteness to the negative.

This question relates to how I presented Antinoos' suicide/death in the Nile, in October of 130 A.D. Historians have argued throughout the centuries as to whether Antinoos took his own life, or was murdered. His burial place is also unknown. (As of this second edition, evidence of his possible burial site has been found at Tivoli, Hadrian's estate a few miles outside Rome, but this conflicts with what you will read later.)

I ask Cathy to see if there is further explanation. Cathy sits quietly at first, then becomes tense and agitated, visibly shaken she begins to report that there is something wrong; she is not feeling well.

"I'm feeling very ill..., my system isn't right..., it's off...,my stomach hurts..., my medicine is not working..., maybe I took too much medication..., maybe I didn't take enough...? I'm tired and confused. I'm so tired..., I'm not feeling well and need to rest..., I need to lie down...,get some sleep and rest..., I can't go on with this..., it's too confusing..., my energy is giving out and I can't stay with this..., I can't go on..., I need to sleep."

Cathy sounds ill, wringing her hands, slumping slightly. We are concerned that she really is sick. It soon becomes apparent that she

45

has gone into trance and is channeling Antinoos. It appears as though she is reporting how he was feeling just before his death. With the last statement, she slumps against the back of the sofa. Nancy calls out Cathy's name, trying to get her to reorient herself, fearing for her wellbeing. Cathy slowly opens her eyes and looks a little surprised as we relate some of the details.

Because the answer to the question of whether Antinoos committed suicide was a clear and emphatic "no", and given that there seemed evidence of illness according to the words said and symptoms described, we speculate that Antinoos' problem may have been a possible food poisoning or an intended poisoning of another nature, perhaps by his own hand. His confusion/concern for what was happening implies that he may have suspected foul play or other machinations which concerned him, making him feel that he was unable to avoid or cope with various intrigues. And this was the groups opinion after a lengthily discussion. Antinoos was murdered by poisoning.

Was Antinoos poisoned by one of the several soothsayers consulted by Hadrian? The Emperor had been concerned about his own health. He had been suffering relapses of an on-going pulmonary condition and experienced periodic hemorrhages. On a journey with Antinoos to visit domains of the eastern regions of the empire, he was warned several times by different seers and sorcerers, of impending death. It had been predicted that his life would be saved and extended by the number of years left, from the life which would be offered up by someone near and dear to him. The stage had been set.

So much more needs investigation, if what was reported at the circle is correct. New characters and intrigues change the story, requiring drastic re-writing. Cathy agreed to continue acting as channel, and we agreed to meet again for this exclusive purpose.

It occurs to several circle members simultaneously that a prime objective of further channeling with the spirit Antinoos would be to clear up the mystery of the location of his burial site. It had been a hope of mine from the beginning, when I first wondered about the possibility of connecting with him.

All that is known is that Hadrian left the boy's body in the hands of the Egyptian priests to be embalmed, a lengthy process taking several months. Hadrian returned to Rome. The record of where Antinoos' body was taken for burial was inscribed on one of the sides of an obelisk, still standing on the Pinchio Hill in Rome. That inscription, however, has been lost to posterity because of a large part of the side containing the information has been obliterated, worn away by movement, time, and the elements. Little remains of the hieroglyphics, making the text incomprehensible. Historians have speculated for centuries, but none know for sure. (As of this 2nd edition, recent archeological discoveries at Hadrian's villa at Tivoli outside Rome suggests the mystery may soon be solved)

We intend to continue circles, with Cathy as a key attendant. She will be available if Antinoos chooses to use her as a channel for the purpose of clarifying the question surrounding his death. This would lead to a more accurate portrayal of the drama, and assure legitimacy of detail. Without this information, my manuscript cannot be complete!

(The novel *Antinoos and Hadrian* has been completed and is available from a major internet book distributor).

UPDATING "A VOICE FROM THE PAST"

In the subsequent months since the above incident of having Antinoos speak through Cathy occurred, the entity has returned several times. There was one attempt from Antinoos, through Nancy. But it was very brief and weak. Having seen the possibility of being able to speak and communicate with him actualize, I decided to accompany Nancy on her yearly trip to Chesterfield, Indiana, the site of the previously mentioned Spiritualist camp. There, during the span of five days I was able to get confirmation of Antinoos' Spirit-Being on several separate occasions, by two different mediums, neither of whom knew the personage of Antinoos, much less details of his life. Compiling the information given to me by the spirit, he did admit to me having died in the Nile, in Egypt. But Antinoos said it had been the result of poisoning. This confirmed Cathy's experience as the medium for Antinoos, at the first channeling. Intrigues were involved, and the specifics of the story were not able to be explored, due to time constraints of our departure. Antinoos was able to answer one of the most important of my questions about his burial place. He was embalmed in Egypt but contrary to the belief of some historians that he was buried in Egypt at Antinoopolis, the city built by Hadrian to honor his favorite's death, or transported to Rome, Antinoos was returned to Claudiopolis, Bithynia. This region was in present-day Turkey. Claudiopolis, Antinoos' city of birth is now called Bolu. It is the reason historians and archaeologists have been unable to locate any site of burial. They have been looking in the wrong places.

Through two separate mediums, separated by two days, this particular piece of information was delivered.

Hoyt Robinette is a medium who works with the trumpet. He also manifests a physical phenomenon that is both amazing and extremely evidential. Hoyt "precipitates" information on blank index cards. This process is as follows. I was one of thirteen people who attended a séance. We sat in a "U" shape around the room with Hoyt sitting in the open top of the letter. I sat close to him on the right. Hoyt broke the seal on a new pack of 3x5 index cards and handed them to me to inspect. I fanned through them to ascertain that there were no markings on either side. He then distributed three levels of cards and numerous capped felt-tipped pens of various colors in a wicker basket which he then covered with a silk scarf. He placed the basket well within sight, two or three feet from where I sat. Hoyt returned to his chair and proceeded to go into trance. The room was in subdued light but everything was perfectly visible. Hoyt began to give messages to everyone in the room. In each case, he mentioned names of loved ones who were present in spirit, and names of guides.

Of the thirteen people, every name was accepted and owned by its recipient. Spirits worked through Hoyt's own guides, and they were able to relate incidences of a personal nature that the medium himself could not have known. The message portion of the séance took almost forty-five minutes. During the time between messages when Hoyt was silent, I could hear a muffled, scratch-like sound coming from the basket. Once done with clarevoyant messages, Hoyt announced that Spirit had also completed the cards. At no time during the messages was the basket moved or touched.

Hoyt got up and removed the kerchief from the basket and emptied the contents, separating cards from pens. He began sorting through the stack, removing those he found to have inscriptions, and handing them to those to whom they were addressed. Each card he

handed out had the name of the person, at the top. Each card contained various names of loved ones and guides, as well as uplifting messages, and many had little bouquets of flowers drawn in the center; each having a different arrangement. One woman who spoke with a German accent was amazed to find the name of a relative, apparently a name that had had a difficult and complex spelling, spelled correctly.

Like the others, my card had my name at the top. It also contained my father's full name, the names of four of my guides, each of which had been brought to me by other mediums the previous days, and to my amazement and joy, the following letters which ran off the edge of the card; "Anti…" It was the only card that contained an uncompleted name. The missing letters did not appear on any other cards as though it may have lain atop another. The name "Antinoos", only partially written, was symbolic for two reasons; his life had been abruptly ended and his story had been only partially told! Through Hoyt, during a direct-voice séance in which I was the only participant, Antinoos came through a second time. The poisoning was confirmed. The site of his death was delivered in these words. "I was buried in the city of my birth. I lie near a great place which is called a cathedral, in your times." I was convinced that this information was incorrect and assumed the medium to be in error or intentionally making something up. After all, in all the research I had done, there had never been a suggestion of Antinoos having been buried at any other location but the two suspected ones. But my belief was challenged and my mind was open to a new possibility.

Patricia Kennedy, another medium of extraordinary ability, brought Antinoos a third time. It was at this session that Antinoos revealed so much, stating his age at death, the country in which he died, and that he had a very "special" kind of relationship with Hadrian, and most importantly in terms of evidential information,

these words…, "I was buried in Bithynia, the place of my birth." Unless Pat was a historian of great knowledge, which she is not, she would have not known this city.

There are some who say that mediums telepathically read the minds of the person who is sitting. If that were the case, both Hoyt and Pat would have mentioned either Egypt or Rome as the burial site. But once again, Bithynia was designated. And upon reflection, it seemed natural that Hadrian would have returned Antinoos to his birthplace, and to his parents. It is also possible that Hadrian had built there, some temple to house or honor Antinoos' remains. History is filled with ancient pagan sites that were subsequently turned into cathedrals and mosques by Christians and Muslims.

As if this were not enough to amaze, when Pat turned to Nancy and brought her Joy Guide, White Lily, who spoke to me by name and said "Now Ray, if you go to page thirty-three of that manuscript you and Nancy are writing, I think you'll find that you have quite a bit of material to change." Nancy and I sat in wonder, not knowing *what* to expect to find on this page! To our amazement when we finally got to manuscript, we saw that the page number was the only page in the entire manuscript that posed the question about Antinoos' death and burial, which were finally answered. No one at Chesterfield had seen the manuscript. It was brought there for Nancy and me to edit during our quiet moments when we were working together in the cafeteria. One more incident to confirm the evidence of my search, and to support my growing confidence in spiritualism! At the breakfast table the following day, while chatting with others, Pat Kennedy suddenly turned to me and asked what significance the number 130, had. She said she believed it to be the date of some significance. This was the year of Antinoos' death. He was found floating in the Nile one early morning in late October of 130 A.D.

So much more needs to be learned. The above information now requires major re-writing of my novel to include the circumstances surrounding causes and reasons for Antinoos' assassination, which will require further channeling.

Importance of Evidential Material

The following incident occurred at the first of four circles conducted by Nancy and me. We hoped to stimulate interest in spiritualism and mediumship by holding a series of classes in southern New Hampshire. The setting was *The Spiral*, a metaphysical book store in Milford, owned by a close friend. (Names have been changed, where necessary, to protect the privacy of those attending).

Prior to beginning the session, Nancy announced that she had had a clear sense of purpose in being there, having resisted cancelling due to illness. She felt compelled to be present. She also reported having had a strong feeling that a spirit indentifying herself as a woman had been present with her in her car, as she drove to the class. The spirit had indentified herself as the sister of someone who would be attending the session.

After a brief period of relaxation exercises and meditation, Nancy started the circle and began with a name heard from her left, near her ear.

"There's a Julia here. Julia Mc…, something like

McCree…. Does anyone recognize a Julia…?"

Until this moment none of the attendants had connected themselves with Nancy's previous comment about her precognition. Robert, a man seated to my left, leaned forward. His voice was excited but cautious.

"I do," Robert responded.

"This is a sister, isn't it?" Nancy's eyes remained closed.

"But her last name is McCree…," Robert sounded strained.

"Nancy's expression looked intense. She seemed locked into the spirit now communicating with her.

"Well…, there's an M beginning the second name."

"It's Julia Marie…, her middle name is Marie!" Robert's voice was filled with emotion and amazement.

Nancy continued. "She's very angry at the way she died! Something awful happened to her, and she is very angry about it."

Robert nodded affirmatively, eyes wide, staring at Nancy. "Yes, she died tragically!"

"I hear the name, 'Arthur'. Does the name Arthur mean anything to you?

"That's her husband."

"Is he in spirit?" Nancy asked.

"No, he is still alive," replied Robert.

Nancy continued concentrating, focused on the impression she was receiving. "There are two boys...,"

Robert could hardly be contained. His voice faltered, on the verge of tears, filled with emotion.

"Yes, they are her sons!"

"Julia wants you to know that she is here, and will be with you. But there is tremendous anger, a sense of outrage."

Robert was unable to participate further, his emotional state made it clear that the contact would best be terminated. He did remain present, but was preoccupied and essentially unable to participate.

The following week found Robert telling us that he had experienced a great peace, after having left our meeting the previous week. He was still amazed at the fact that the information had been disclosed, and asked Nancy several times, "How do you know all that?" Robert continues to be in awe, but believes his sister is actually communicating from spirit.

Nancy confirmed the fact that Robert' sister felt as though she had been left to die, that her family had failed to rescue her as they had so many times before. Her sense of outrage revolved around the feeling of being abandoned. She had not wanted to die, even though she had taken her own life! Through Nancy, Julia said "Peety knows…" Robert said the name "Peety" belonged to his nephew and uncle in spirit, and to a pet parakeet Julia had once owned as a child. The meaning of the message was left unanswered. Nancy mentioned another name she felt Julia had impressed upon her. Robert was surprised and stated that until that very week, it had been unknown to him. But he had recently received a phone call from a man who identified himself with the same name and the nature of the call was much too personal to divulge, but assured us that it was certainly meaningful, and understood why it had been introduced. Spirit messages may often have great value to the one for whom the message is intended, but may appear meaningless to others.

Nancy continued explaining that Julia wanted Robert to know she was present; that she was pleased with Robert's attendance and interest in Spiritualism, and that she would remain with him. It is likely that this spirit will return to further clarify the circumstances of her death. Through this experience, Robert is assured of his sister's continued existence, and Julia herself, is able to grow in spirit by being able to process the heavy burden of such a tragic situation. Nancy stated that since Julia's death three years ago, she had been healing in Spirit, and just as she was a nurse on the Earth plane, she is now working to help people who also pass through suicide. Healing of the dead and living is served!

Open Mind and Integrity

The aspects of personal development, aesthetic fulfillment, and professional enhancement all contribute to my on-going interest in

Spiritualism. By taking risks and giving out impressions I feel, and having most of them validated, each week brings confirmation. Those who tell of their first experience in a circle all relate a reluctance to give their impressions out of fear of being wrong. It was my fear, also.

There is much to understand about developing mediumship. The first is to acknowledge that we are trying to be open and receptive to those messages being given by spirits. This is like trying to send out a radio signal with rudimentary equipment and attempting to pick up the broadcast with an equally primitive receiver, all the while trying to perceive the message which is being distorted and interrupted by many other signals filling the air-waves.

It is for this reason that being relaxed, balanced, tuned, and having the proper energy is so important. The composition of the group meeting in the circle can have much to do with the meeting's success. Any negativism or animosity, anyone attending who might be emotionally distraught, can reduce the circle's energy and even set up a barrier between those meeting and the spirits trying to get through. As in any human interaction, it is not always possible to bring a group of people together who blend or who are simpatico.

A circle develops characteristics and a personality of its own, and that becomes evident. It may be necessary to structure a group so that the best elements of all members are utilized to make the circle's energy and dynamics, optimal. Even those who are new and think they bring little to the circle, help to charge it with their own psychic energy, and therefore act as batteries. All who participate take responsibility for what happens during the encounter.

Religion and Spiritualism

Those whom I have met who are fully involved in Spiritualism and make it a practice to attend a few churches located north of

Boston, keep their religion to themselves. Although they share their experiences and thoughts with those they know who are of the same beliefs and inclinations, they do not seek converts. Unlike so many religious organizations, there is in Spiritualism an absence of exclusiveness and religious intolerance towards other faiths. These aspects of religious intolerance and punitive beliefs are what separate *"true"* religious (spiritual) faiths from those that allow humans to **be** human and accept the idea that life is filled with complexity…, the wonderful gift all of us initially inherit. This is what is especially and exceptionally appealing about spiritualism. Spiritualism has nothing to do with converting the world to its view. It does deal with personal and internal development and fulfillment, with no compelling force to drop cherished belief systems in order to accept spiritualistic philosophy, a quality much absent in most faiths.

My experience with spiritualism and with those who practice it is that they do not proselytize, but are content with communicating with others of similar interests. People who believe in spiritualism move about the world quietly, willing to allow those who believe differently than they do, their choice. This is a remarkably fresh approach to religion and theological philosophy. The temple of worship is wherever those who chose to, gather. There is no need for a church structure, although many do exist.

In having discussed my recent circle experience with friends and acquaintances, some have reacted with skepticism. Some have even wondered about my sanity for believing that the spirits of departed relatives or known people could communicate with the living. Yet some of these very people find no irony in their own religious beliefs of communicating with dead relatives, friends, or saints, and do so daily through prayer or other forms of dialogue. One individual's religious beliefs and rituals are almost always another's superstitions.

My Beginning

After a number of conversations Nancy and I shared during the first two years we worked together a few hours a week at a residential half-way house, she asked if I might be interested in partaking in her weekly circle. Her straightforward manner, genuineness and honesty had led me to respect her as a caring and forthright person. She had told me her history of having been born into a Spiritualist family and having been raised in the teachings.

I was intrigued.

I was ready.

I attended.

I continue to do so. My understanding grows. Our recent discussions revealed a mutual interest in getting our thoughts on paper, and developing a manual which would define spiritualism and explain the purpose of a circle; how to convene and conduct one. The decision to move forward with this project has been rewarding and enlightening.

The further purpose of knowledge led me to Bill Rowan and Ramon.

CHAPTER FIVE
Ramon Speaks

Bill Rowan is a medium from Australia who once conducted a home circle to which I had been invited. The host, who knew I was working on a book on the subject of home circles, thought it would be interesting and to my advantage to hear him. It certainly was! The following is a transcription of the words of Ramon, a spirit who is channeled by Mr. Rowan.

"Good evening! Let me introduce myself. My name is Ramon, and of course it is one of a multiplicity of names that I have had, but utilize only as an identification of the persona I present you. What I should like to do this evening is ask you to come with me on a short journey to 1848, and find the beginning of what is termed as Modern Spiritualism.

"Most of you know this. Forgive me for repeating. What happed was that there was another breakthrough made between our conscious level (spirit world) and the physical level which you inhabit. The idea was to present people with the information that contained within themselves, is one small particle of God. It was not necessary for Spirits to create a church to realize that this could be so. If they, (people on the earth plane) sat together in home circles, communication took place and that there was a simplicity in the fact that it did. It was only later, as people began to understand or feel that there should be organizations that unfortunately, coming together in small groups, was set aside. And of course, equally, as organizations grew, rules and regulations were set down which said *this* is the *only* way communication can take place.

"The simplicity was lost. What is not being done is that through a concerted effort of many of us, we are hoping that people will begin to see that when we come together and you come together, people will be able to raise their consciousness to the extent to which they are able to not only contact us, but contact the higher properties of their own being. Now let me explain that more fully. People speak of various levels of consciousness, or planes of being. But this is unfortunately untrue. There are no planes such as one, two, or three levels. There are multiple levels of consciousness which are all equally powerful at the present time. Because contained in you, in true fact is a spirit replica of the physical body. People call this the etheric body or astral body. We prefer the term spirit body.

When you sleep it emerges from the physical and becomes the liaison officer between the higher part of your consciousness and the physical part of your being. And you can find, as you will, that if you sit together in this way and blend your thoughts together, then you can start to sense and emerge from the confinement of the physical body and start to experience in physical awakening, the fact that you are not just a physical body but a spirit consciousness as well.

"For simplicity sake, again, accept if you will that there are three levels of consciousness in which you are operating in this physical life. By sitting quietly and assuming a posture which allows you to relax as fully as you can, you create passivity in your mind which then makes you aware of the light which is contained within you. And you expand that light! And you embrace in doing so, the multiplicity of levels of consciousness in which you are operative. You draw to you individuals such as ourselves who seek to help you understand that this physical life is just a miniscule part of the totality of life which you have known and will continue to live.

"Each of you has lived again and again with different persona and in different realms. You have experienced life to its greatest degree. You will find that there are records of all that has happened (which people call the Akashic records). And apart from that, you have a record of your own lifetimes; all the experiences which have been gained on the many journeys which have been taken as part of a souls structure to which you belong, literally like the higher consciousness.

"Again, by sitting down quietly and tuning in and tapping those records you can begin to see who you are, what you are, and what purposes to which you have been sent as you walk along this particular pathway which has been allotted to you. A time will come when all people will again be conscious of this. It is something which has happened before.

"In the beginning of time, as far as humanity was concerned,

beings took part in the expansion of consciousness in brute forms that were humanoid and sent them along the pathway so that at times vast civilizations have been created by humankind and destroyed by humankind because they remembered the animalistic part of their nature. What is seen, however, is that a step has been taken that has been an Ascension toward the time in which again, humanity en-mass will realize that they are an integral part of each other. That, because that is so, what they do is important and if they harm another being, then they harm themselves. This is true and simple!

"Look at this clearly. The many religious beliefs which have been part of humankind's endeavors have, unfortunately, too often bound humanity to the wheel. Had they not existed, humankind would have remembered how they were capable of acting in such a way that this life could be a veritable Garden of Eden which is said it was, at one time.

"However, we return to the present day! In the past decade you have each seen how the efforts which have been made by those we call *The Hierarchy*, are taking effect, where people are beginning break down the barriers which have parted them from their own people. Begin to see how stupid it is to act in that way so that they are divisions of land and people. You begin to understand that in this technological age it is still possible to reach out and touch each other.

"Let me for a moment, speak of this technological age and speak of the simplistic ways that communication took place in 1848 and from that period of time. You have advanced into a vast technological age where humankind is sending rockets out into pace in an endeavor to find life beyond the reaches of this small galaxy. It is a small galaxy! And of course we are also interested in using that technology you have created as a result of which experiments have been carried out so to that voices are being heard upon tape recorders where no apparent sounds should exist. People have said that it might even be possible for us to show a replica of ourselves using your television sets. But think of the danger involved in such a production. People would then tune in, as it were, to the friends and relatives not only daily, but every moment of the day, particularly of those they have loved and lost.

"The purpose of communication would be defeated. However, what is now currently being done is that scientists on your physical level are experimenting with lasers so that in time to come, we, in our etheric form, will be seen clearly without the need of having a materializing medium present. And when that is done, advances will have been made to such a degree that literally all people will be able to see us as we truly are. The only difference between ourselves and you is that we live in an infinite body.

"The vibratory rate of that body is so fine that it cannot be seen by the normal physical sight which is yours. Let me ask you to consider a wheel with spokes. It revolves so fast that the spokes are invisible but if you reach out and touch them, you find that they do exist. We literally walk through you at times, and that is why you feel, as they say, a cold shiver going through you! You equally walk through us because our bodies are so much finer. And you might sense and feel that we are there. If you sit down quietly and try to attune to that feeling then hopefully you start to experience the beginnings of mediumship.

"For a moment, let me digress. Let me assume that all of you are interested in developing some form of mediumship. It is most unlikely that using the sight and the hearing that you have physically, you will see and hear us. But a mental attunement, a telepathic communication that we can form with you can be so clear and concise that you can justify saying that you are seeing and hearing us.

"At all times, remember one thing above all others; that the purpose behind developing mediumship is not to advance yourselves, not to create for yourselves a place where you are recognized by your peer group or others as extra-ordinary. But rather, that you care about people and accordingly care for people. Because true mediumship is the ability to care for people to such a degree that you can help them realize that *death is but an interlude in life*! Life is a continuum and we say that you will experience it again and again, which causes me to give this view on it. You can not be judgmental! You may have walked the same way as those you seek to judge!

61

YOU, THE MEDIUM

You can discern in them what is happening. You can make such clarity of your discernment that you will not make the mistakes that other people seem to have made.

"You can say to yourself, I am one with God and as long as this is so, there are no difficulties which I cannot overcome, no problems too great for me, no way in which it can be said I am not part of the creative force. There is this creative force within you. It merely evidences itself in many ways by the utilization of gifts which are understood on this level; the gift of painting art, the gift of music, the gift of listening, the gift of teaching, and hopefully, also the gift of feeling, the gift of clairvoyance, clairaudience…, these many gifts which are associated with mediumship. For those of you who each act in such a way that you discern the possibilities within you to become a medium, I simply say this. Believe in yourself. Have such confidence in what you are doing that it becomes a part of what you are and in tune with the infinite!

"Be with God!"

A SECOND READING FROM RAMON

The above communication with the entity, Ramon, channeled by Bill Rowan, raised so many questions about the conducting of circles and how Spirit might seek to guide us that it became obvious more contact was needed. Almost a year after the initial reading, we sent a copy of the transcribed first reading to Bill, in Australia, with the additional queries. Far beyond our expectations, the following material was sent back. The sessions was conducted with Bill Rowan channeling "Ramon", and facilitated by two of Bill's colleagues, Mark and Margaret. The extent to which Bill assisted us demonstrates his friendly and cooperative nature.

Ramon: At this time, since it has been asked that we respond in part to this epistle which has been sent forward, I should like to do exactly that. Is that acceptable?

Margaret: The letter written by Ramond Berube, states that they have a circle already going and that they sit twice a week. They want to know what you and the other spirits (she actually referred to Ramon and the other

spirits as "the gang"), think of home circles. How they are compared with church groups. It looks like they are also asking what is the purpose of home circles and how should they be conducted so that people could come closer to the goals and objectives that you all would hope they were working toward, in these groups.

Ramon: To this, firstly let's go back to the time in which it was said that the advent of modern Spiritualism took place with the happenings in the Fox cottage and the communications which then took place between Charles B Rosna and the Fox family, and eventually with neighbors and friends. At that time, communication took place by percussive sounds which were created through the energies supplied by their spirit intervention which was occurring. Over a period of time as people became conscious of the fact that communication could take place, then home circles, as they are termed, were set up. And the simplicity of what was done was very important at that time. No rules and regulations were imposed to prevent the communication from taking place. And invariably it was found that as a home circle was formed, at least one member of the family showed mediumistic tendencies and became the focal point through whom, then, the communication could take place.

The purpose of home circles is to provide the focal point and to discover in one or more members of the circle an ability created whereby communication can take place without hindrance. In effect what is needed is that, first, people come together in small groups consisting of eight or ten individuals..., usually, hopefully, family members or close friends. The intention then, is to have them create harmony amongst themselves and to patiently exercise the ability to relax and be open in their attitude that they are receptive of the impressions that can be given to them by their spirit helpers.

As a group is formed, one could say that it becomes like a light-house and it sends out beacons or prisms of light which attracts individuals from our level of consciousness, who are interested in utilizing the vehicle of expression which then can be found. In time, if the harmony is built up completely, then the individuals in that group and collectively become conscious of the identity of their specific helpers. A bridge of

communication is formed which becomes very, very strong indeed so that as times goes forward, possibly they can venture into what is called physical phenomena whereby materialization or direct voice can take place.

Naturally it is oft times difficult for people to accept the fact that there can be a bridge of communication between one level of consciousness and another. And so a belief needs to be instilled in the group that this is a prime requisite to be looked for in the following bridge of communication. Because the group is limited in numbers, then whatever evidential value it had oft times, is contained within the group and limited perspective. In that regard, then, supposedly ideal conditions can be set up and communications established. What should be looked at is that correspondence can be struck between one group and another.

In the years from 1930 to around 1950 in the United Kingdom, one individual, Noah Zevdin, attempted exactly that; to form communicative abilities between one group and another. Within the past few years Noah has in fact communicated with individuals within the United Kingdom. A society called Noah's Ark Society has been formed specifically with the intention of bringing back what circles have lost, the abilities to act or have physical mediumship take place.

Let me recap the fact that in the initial stages of the formation of spiritualism as such, all communication which took place was through physical phenomena. Gradually, however, that went by the wayside and mental mediumship took over. Mental mediumship is now still far more prevalent and still, oft times, has even greater impact than some of the physical phenomenon which took place.

Now as far as Raymond's question is concerned, in so far as their group is to be looked at, the potential which is to be found there can lead them along avenues in which physical phenomenon can take place, but that coordinated with strong mental mediumship so that the guidance which it receives will be valid in itself. If something can be done by him and his companion, Nancy, it should be to that effect that they can establish concrete recognition of the intervention which is taking place between themselves and their helpers.

From that point of time, then, view the increased activity which is

taking place as an encouragement which can be given to other groups of like nature. They will have information which will help them in that regard.

Now please, Margaret, are there any other questions in that regard?

Margaret: The letter seems to be questioning whether there should be some sort of structure in these groups so that, in a sense following a certain structure makes for an easier exchange of data. Or whether by doing that, they fall into the trap of being like an organized religion and losing their spontaneity.

Ramon: This is one thing that should be avoided as far as possible: accepting the idea that spiritualism is a religion. It is a method of having communication between different levels of consciousness. *Religious beliefs truly have no part to play in the formation of this bridge of communication of which we speak.* Whoever is part of a group activity has the right to believe as they wish as far as their religious principles are concerned. But they should not be, or become the basis of communication. One of the reasons that it is so is because we have looked aghast at the misinformation which has been fed to and accepted by individuals with strong religious beliefs which have in fact and to a degree, destroyed the communicable level which was being affected.

Am I making this quite clear?

Margaret: Yes. I'd like to extend that just a tad further to say, okay, no formal structure as such but is there some sort of procedure that could evolve that would put them more on the path of achieving spiritual development? I have the feeling that there are some of them that want to focus more on the development of the spiritual rather than the psychic stuff. Is there more of a procedure that they could think about so that they could facilitate that development more?

Ramon: Let us say that a group has been formed with the intention of having communication take place between one level and the other. As has been said, it is necessary for any communication to take place to have receptivity in the individuals who are part of the group. What should be looked at is that those of us who seek to communicate, should be regarded as friends who have called in to exchange information with the people who are forming the group. And because that is so, there has to be not only an

acceptance of the fact that it can take place, but a recognition of the fact that we *are* friends, *and friends do not preach to each other!*

YOU, THE MEDIUM

Margaret: Again, extending from that, it's safe to say that you should fix the attitude first; agree that you all are meeting for everyone's well-being and then let happen naturally whatever comes to pass whatever the mood is. If someone has a problem and that becomes the topic of the night, let it happen. If everyone wishes to talk about love, or whatever, let it happen, letting whatever the mood of the session come through rather than following a specific structure as such.

Ramon: Let's begin with the formation of the group. Sit comfortably as a circle. In so doing, the prime requisite is to have harmony among the members of the group and to invite communication to take place either on the mental or physical level. The group should meet together regularly, which is of tremendous importance to begin, because since we have no true concept of the passage of time, then we must attend to the sensation of acknowledgement of time passing of the individuals in the group. Because that is so, we should insist on a time to start and finish the group activities. In other words, if it is decided that the group meets at 7pm, it should be at that time on the dot, as they say, because we would be then in attendance at that time. That having been established, the group is met together and if they like asking for intervention through prayer, then that can be done.

With the recognition of having in their consciousness the idea that they were forming a bridge of communication to quiet a number, prayer would lift their own consciousness, that is, prayer to a Universal Spirit, God-concept, whichever it might be; lift their consciousness and then attract individuals of like mind. It should also be established, that is, there is a need for them to know who the guiding light or force is to be within the group post. They can postulate the idea that they are to be attracted by or to a specific individual or characteristic of that individual. What is preferable however, is that as one or other of them enhances this sensitivity, and then it will be invariably found that they can act as a spokesman for the entity or personage that is making contact.

Once that is done, then the rest of the group should focus attention on helping that sensitive to become truly the focal point through which

communication is enhanced and established. And after a period of time in which this is done, as has been said, they will begin to depend on and accept the information which is given; instructions which can be given to perfect the happenings in their own group.

Margaret: What you seem to be saying is that they should not worry about developing or communicating with other groups. They have to develop their own group first. Then they will be more confident that people will appear, like you're saying, and the groups will form networks on their own. Perhaps they need to develop that core structure to quite a degree, and then think about connecting to another group.

Ramon: This is preferable and desirable because unless they have pertinent information drawn *to* them by their own interaction with the spirit helpers, then they cannot justifiably say "this is how things can be done". Not *should be done*, but *can be done!*.

In other words, Margaret, let's say that you had an ability. You would have to be able to show that ability before you could ask anyone else to look at what you've done and perhaps be able to say to themselves, we can follow your footsteps.

Margaret: I think that's the next piece, Ramon. What they are hoping to achieve is not just on par with a university degree, so that if you get your piece of paper then, yes you do exchange information. This is far more spiritual! Therefore, you don't necessarily need to establish a network on the same sort of understanding. It is something quite special, and it may be many years before that group are sufficiently confident within their own talents, to expand. Because until they develop that talent, it may be that they don't need to network and they build a center on their own where they are, and people just come to them.

Yet, that's elaborating a bit on what you're saying. Do you want to respond to that, Ramon?

Ramon: Let us say, at this time, that it is very essential that the confidence in the communication is established so that their helpers draw close and they begin to know them and the idiosyncrasies, that they can start to accept the advice which undoubtedly will be given as to how their own group should operate for the best results to be achieved. Once that confidence

and ability is gained, then they will find, in a comparatively short span of time that the results they might look for can be more readily achieved. And of course the prime purpose in having a home circle is to establish that communication, with definite results. Once those results are achieved satisfactorily, then they can start communicating with others and find that they have perhaps achieved similar results, or have taken steps to advance their abilities to a greater degree so that an interchange of their ideas can be promulgated and accepted.

Margaret: Then what you are saying is that it is a good idea to establish fixed times so that they get a pattern going. Perhaps I can ask that, when you mention that basically the circle forms from a group of friends, then from them would emerge the medium. Perhaps they are asking whether there is supposed to be some level of commitment at the beginning, from these groups, so that when Nancy and Raymond announce that they will have readings at this time, anybody who wants, can come. Or do they just say "these are the times the meetings are! If you come or not come, fine!", and allow the group itself to develop. Maybe people will drop out and others will come in. Or should it be that there is much more of a firm commitment between them.

Ramon: That is an important question. And it is very, very necessary for it to be understood that from our side, quite often a necessary sifting out needs to take place before the complete harmony required can be induced in a group. Since that is so, then let's say a group of eight people have come together. If it is found that even one of the group is not able to enter into harmonious communication on the physical level, then there is less likelihood that they could have harmonious communication on our level.

So we take steps to see either that they cannot attend religiously; forgive the pun, or there are happenings which take place that make it impossible for them to achieve the results they are looking for, to look at the need to establish regularity in their presence within the group. Of course there will be times due to illness or other unfortunate events one or another cannot be part of the group. But that is accepted and prepared for, in a sense on our side so that the group is existent, the chair in which that individual normally sits should be left in that space, empty, with the

understanding that the spirit-consciousness of that person can be there. So the harmony of the group is held and maintained.

Let it be said here, that it is very unlikely that the happenings in any group will have world-shattering events take place. It was hoped that in the inducement of spiritualism, as it is called, that it could become in a sense, not world-shattering but have revelations which could apply to humanity en-mass. It was a break-through, one of many which have taken place. And it is still possible that the ideas which are promulgated can be like a seed planted in someone's consciousness whereby they can see that they are part of a harmonious world, and the continuity of life.

So let me, finally, in speaking of home circles, ask Raymond and those of his group, or whatever group he attends, to understand this; the actual necessity to meet regularly at a time they designate. To try to the best of their ability to be at peace with each other. And then when that is accomplished, there is a greater likelihood of spirit intervention taking place to the extent in which they can be then directed and guided to the goals which they hope might be achieved. The rest, as they say, will follow on!

I must also ask it to be understood that what I have said before is correct; that like attracts like. If they are in the hope that they will have exalted personages at their séances, then they might well be deflated by finding that with such a hope, the imaginative qualities run wild and they have mischievous contacts which are made. Use, as they say, common sense. Question what is taking place. Do not be misled by extraneous sounds being put down to the intervention by and with spirit people. At all times be on guard against allowing the imagination to run wild.

Communication has already been established, but more dependence on the validity of that communication is something to aim for. In time when the book, as it will be, is published, they will undoubtedly have communication from people on the physical level who will relay information about their own development in groups. Then, will be established the link which is to take place!"

This ended Ramon's talk on the nature of mediumship and reasons for seeking development. Ramon made it quite clear, through Bill Rowan,

that each of us has the ability to develop already existing gifts, that this in fact, is a responsibility and those in spirit are waiting for us, waiting for the moment of realization, perhaps as a result of their urging, for us to become the means by which they can give us knowledge and allow us to speak once again with loved ones who are present but exists in a different form. The home circle offers an excellent opportunity to explore and experience the wonders of mediumship!

The following chapter will help the reader understand Ramon's historical references. For Spiritualism has a significant place in history!

CHAPTER SIX
History of Spiritualism

There are two meanings to the word "spiritualism". The first is a metaphysical reference to a nonmaterial world of spirits common to most religions. But another meaning refers to a doctrine that believes it is possible to communicate with the spirits of those who have died, and of those social institutions that hold that tenet. Implicit, therefore, is the belief that there is a life after death, not a belief unique to the Spiritualist doctrine.

Belief in after-life is not only a part of Christian doctrine but is also found within countless other religions, both ancient and modern. What sets Spiritualism apart from the more conventional religious beliefs is the practice of speaking with those who have gone into spirit and the acknowledgement that it is an ordinary occurrence, not a novelty, without notoriety.

Andrew Jackson Davis, one of the early proponents of spiritualism, in 1847 published *Nature's Divine Revelations*, a book still widely read in which he states that on the death of the physical body, the human spirit remains alive and moves on to one or another of a considerable range of worlds or "spheres" where it commences yet another stage of existence. Since the spirit itself has not died, but exists with full consciousness, there is no reason to suppose that it could not make itself known. Ironically, Spiritualists claim to do no more than demonstrate as fact, what Christians are expected to believe without question; that the human personality (soul) survives bodily death. Peter Roche de Coppens, professor of sociology and anthropology at East Stroudsburg University, states in his book *Divine Light and Fire: Practicing Esoteric Christianity*: "Each person has a destiny in this world, and when the right time arrives this destiny will be made manifest. Also, there are spiritual powers that watch over us and that will arrange

71

encounters, situations, and experiences. Thus, to be true to one's self and one's destiny is important – then to work, patiently, upon oneself as to know and perfect oneself in such a way that when the right moment and opportunities do present themselves one can recognize them and make the best of them. There are invisible worlds as well as invisible beings and it is in the invisible worlds that the true causes originate. We are never left alone or truly abandoned. There are spiritual beings that watch over us and that help our evolution and becoming".

Belief in the after-life and spiritualistic-type practices have been a part of numerous cultures throughout history. Reincarnation is mentioned in the Old and New Testaments. Emperor Constantine deleted references to reincarnation contained in the New Testament in A.D. 325, as a sign of the religious thinking of the times. In A.D. 553, the Second Council of Constantinople confirmed this action and declared the concept a heresy. Reincarnation offered an opportunity to correct the wrongs of this life by returning in another and that limited the power of the Church, for it allowed too much time for the faithful to seek salvation.

The record of materialization séance is preserved in the account in the Old Testament of Saul's visit to the witch or medium of Endor, in the course of which a materialization appeared which was regarded by the king as the prophet Samuel (I Sam. Xxviii, 7-19). References to the concept of life-after-death are also found in the Gospel of Thomas (The Twin), in which Thomas relates the sayings of Jesus. (Saying 18) "The followers said to Jesus, 'Tell us how our end will be." Jesus said. "Have you discovered the beginning, then, so that you are seeking the end? For where the beginning is, the end will be. Fortunate is one who stands at the beginning! That one will know the end and will not taste death"
(Saying 19) Jesus said, "Fortunate is one who came into being before coming into being. "
"If you become my followers and listen to my sayings, these stones will serve you.
"For there are five trees in paradise for you; they do not change, summer or winter, and their leaves do not fall. Whoever knows them will not taste death."

Throughout the middle ages there are reports of mediumistic phenomena in witch-trial documents, and it is safe to assume that many who were persecuted and put to death for witchcraft were what would now be called mediums. The spirits with which they might have communicated were believed to be demons. Some mediums were found to be possessed by the devil because there were reported to demonstrate the phenomena of speaking in tongues (languages unknown to the speaker), and levitations. Contacts with spirits is also a reported phenomena in Native American Indian cultures in which direct communications were possible with animal spirits and other spirits associated with elements of nature as well as with those of departed ancestors.

The Fox Sisters

Although spiritualism seems to have been practiced extensively by many cultures and religions from early times, it was almost unknown in modern civilized society until March 1848.

On that date odd happenings began at a farmhouse in a small town in New York State. The daughters of a man named Fox, were disturbed by raps that seemed unaccountable. The youngest daughter Kate, and her sister Margaret, challenged the supposed spirit to repeat the number of times she gestured silently with her fingers. Communication was established and a code developed by which raps given could answer questions. The spirit indentified himself as a peddler who had been murdered in the house by a previous owner, and whose belongings had been stolen, and the body buried in the dirt cellar. Slater Brown reports in his book *The Heyday of Spiritualism*, that upon attempted investigation of the dirt cellar that was dug up a number of times, continuously filled up with seepage water. The search was given up. Later after another dig, bones and some hair were found along with the remains of a tattered knapsack said to belong to the peddler, who had indicated its existence. It was never proven conclusively that the bones and hair were human remains.

As the knocks continued and as neighbors spread the word, large gatherings became commonplace, and the girls were carefully scrutinized by a host of community leaders and well-known personalities. Most who spent their time in séances and interviewing the Fox sisters, came away convinced that the sounds were made by something unaccountable, but certainly not by the girls.

Sitting for spirit communication spread rapidly from that time. The Fox sisters devoted much of their lives to acting as mediums in this country and in England, and were followed by many other mediums.

Emanuel Swedenborg

Predating the Fox sisters by almost a hundred years was a man who Slater Brown describes as being responsible for the revival of spiritualist interests:

The resurgence of popular belief in a spiritual world that is eternal, infinite, primary, and the ultimate home of all mortals was mainly due to Emanuel Swedenborg, whose works were translated from Latin into English were beginning to exert an influence during the first quarter of the nineteenth century.

Swendenborg, born January 29, 1688, was a Swedish scientist, philosopher, and theologian who was greatly respected in his country as a learned men of letters. He was educated at Upsala University and traveled the continent for five years in search of scientific and mechanical knowledge. He was the author of numerous scientific works, and publisher of periodicals.

"…Swedenborg was engaged in anatomical and physiological studies. As he had sought to find the "soul" of creation in pure motion, he now sought to understand the soul of man and to find it in its own kingdom, which is his body" (Encyclopedia Britannica). Once embarked on theological studies, he began to lose the respect of those who had admired his scientific brain. Swedenborg ascertained that his turn to this area of study was a response to a divine vision, and that this vision initiated a quest that lasted for the remainder of his life. Swedenborg stated without reserve that he could be in both the spiritual world and in this world, consciously, and that the long works produced during this time were not of his own creation but from the spirit world; a revelation from God. The peculiar twist in this situation was that unlike the spiritualism of today in which the spirit is "admitted" into the material world, Swedenborg's belief was that he had been admitted into the spiritual world. Slater Brown describes Swedenborg's influence on the future interest in spiritualism in this manner:

> Swedenborg's most widely read book, *Heaven and Hell*, had appeared in English as early as 1772, but it was not until the early years of the nineteenth century that it found it's public. Meanwhile Swedenborgian churches had begun to appear in spite of the fact that Swedenborg seems never to have approved of the idea and made no effort to establish a church himself. The first one, called the Church of the New Jerusalem, was founded in England six years after his death in 1772, and in 1792 a church was organized in America.

Swedenborg seemed little concerned about his captivity of communicating with spirits. He did express caution for others, seeing danger in their being misled by spirits who might have dubious intent and untrustworthy purposes. He believed himself divinely chosen and advised that only those like-chosen could conduct spirit communication safely.

> When spirits begin to speak with a man, he must be aware that he believes nothing that they say. For nearly everything they say is fabricated by them, and they lie; for if they are permitted to narrate anything, as what heaven is, an how things in heaven are to be understood, they would tell so many lies that a man would be astonished. This they would do without solid affirmation.... Wherefore men must beware and not believe them. It is on this account that the state of speaking with spirits on this earth is most perilous.

In the 1830's a Frenchman named Alphonse Cahagnet fell under the influence of Swedenborg after reading *Heaven and Hell*. Charged by Swedenborg's details of heaven, and the apparent confirmation that a future life and spirits existed, he became involved with several people who seemed to have mediumship qualities. One of these was a young woman with whom he had been working, using the process of magnetizing to cure her of sleepwalking, discovering that she had clairvoyant powers. Adele Magnot provided descriptions of deceased relatives of people she did not know. The accuracy of her reports, confirmed time and again by both believers and skeptics, was reported by Cahagnet in his second volume, *Celestial Telegraph*. More than forty cases are recorded of her contacts with spirits in which depictions of personal characteristics, some in great detail, describing clothing, mannerisms, physical deformities, led Cahagnet to offer these as evidential proof. Cahagnet's recorded séances are of historical importance, as they are among the first recorded and witnessed events which offered verified data.

Andrew Jackson Davis

Andrew Jackson Davis, born in Blooming Grove, New York, on August 11, 1826, was the son of an alcoholic cobbler. Andrew had received the equivalent of about five months of formal education, and had made little effort to educate himself. At the age of nineteen he authored *The Principles of Nature, Her divine Revelations and a Voice to Mankind*, an 800 page book which Spirit dictated through him while he was in trance. This work has such detailed knowledge of astronomy, archeology, geology, and a remarkable understanding of biblical history, that it could only have been written by someone literate, well educated, with a mind well developed in philosophy and theology. Yet those who knew him as a young man and in his later years agree that he was never serious in reading or study. Out of trance, Davis appeared extremely limited. By his own admission, Davis felt so strongly that this material was not his, that he was merely a medium through which the information was passed to the world by spirits that he agreed to relinquish all profit from the book's sales.

The Davenport Brothers

To a large degree, much of what people think about and associate with spiritualism, unusual occurrences, the movement of articles, the appearance of hands or objects, was popularized by the Davenport

brothers. Born in Buffalo, N.Y., Ira and William began to exhibit their skills in 1855 when they were introduced to the public. They were sixteen and fourteen years old. Their mediumship was discovered shortly after they had read about wrappings and spirit communications in the newspapers. Rappings began to disrupt the family gatherings at the table, and there are unobserved reports of the brothers and a younger sister floating around the room. These reports of levitation are not taken seriously however.

Soon notables from various social circles were attending séances, and demonstrations were being done at private gatherings. A major feat was for the brothers to be placed in a large specially-built wooden container, and tied with multiple knots and finally secured to benches located at opposite ends of the box. They would emerge within minutes, freed. Reentering, the ropes scattered on the container floor, within minutes a signal would indicate the doors to be opened to reveal the brothers fully tied. The knots were so intricate and carefully tied, at some points that it would have been impossible for either to reach; it seemed obvious to all that something other than human intervention was involved. Often, while secured and locked within those cabinets, with a variety of musical instruments that had been placed on the floor, the sound of notes followed by simple melodies would be heard.

The Davenport's amazing performances were reported in full detail by newspapers, and also were recorded by numerous doctors, scientists, and other notables. Most judged that what they had seen, seemed to be authentic. These public spectacles did much to promote interest in spiritualism, but also added to the notoriety of what many felt were tricks and illusions. Those less scrupulous saw opportunity for taking advantage of those people who, because of a variety of needs, wanted to believe in spirits and other things supernatural. The proliferation of practitioners of spiritualism and séances spread throughout the United States and Europe.

Controversy

The second half of the nineteenth century saw an alienation of most professionals, who had come to spiritualism with interests and curiosity about physical manifestations and phenomena. Those few spiritualists who

proved to be honest and whom no hoax could be detected, were overshadowed by the many who took on the mantel of medium for profit and deception. But for the majority who flocked to spiritualism the motivation for this activity was varied. Many were simply curious and fascinated with the supernatural. Others had a more serious intent of convincing themselves of life after death, as confirmation of their traditional religious beliefs. Some, suffering the loss of loved ones and wishing for solace and consolation, sought the services of mediums to communicate with them and retain a connection. Others wanted information about a future life. Believers united in groups and clubs, organized into spiritualistic associations and churches to better support themselves as a group and for spiritual reinforcement.

These new associations were not allowed to exist without opposition. Verbal condemnation and mob violence were popular reactions to novel ideas and beliefs not shared by the majority, who suspected fraud or evil. The suspicion of evil was fueled by Christian churches that feared that new revelations and newly established Spiritualist Churches would supplement or replace Christian revelation. Some religious bodies also saw spiritualist practice as forbidden activity or necromancy. The Holy Office of the Roman Catholic Church in 1898, condemned spiritualistic practice, but allowed legitimate scientific investigation of mediumship phenomena.

Simultaneous with the irrational obstructions by Christian churches to the new interests in spiritualism, there was an enthusiastic acceptance, often uncritical, by those who had lost their faith in traditional Christianity. They were offered a belief system based not on myth or proof of faith, but on facts observable by anyone. The facts were given through mediumship.

Forms of Mediumship

There are several kinds of spiritual communication: (1) mental mediumship such as trance, (2) production of materializations and other forms of physical mediumship, including spirit photography, and (3) spirit healing.

Mental mediumship essentially results in messages from spirits of the departed. These messages may be directed to loved ones present or absent,

or may be information about conditions beyond the grave. Several mediums have been the source through which spirits have directed books of fiction, history, or manuals for the purpose of teaching. It has been noted by many who have witnessed such presentations, that some mediums experience dramatic transformations of voice, facial structure and body positions, sometimes while in trance.

In the phenomena of physical mediumship, the playing of musical instruments, transport of physical objects (apports), levitation of the medium, or surrounding raps, have sometimes been considered too theatrical and too much like horseplay to be the activities of spirits. They are, however, considered of value by many for providing evidence of the reality of the spiritual activity. A phenomenon considered important by spiritualists is the appearance of a filmy substance called ectoplasm, which is a quasi-material substance derived from the body of the medium which may take the form of a face or hand or compete body. Such materializations have been photographed, although some put forth as genuine photos of spirits, have been proven to have been constructed of cheesecloth. Still, some have stood the test and are thought to be genuine. Spirit photographs have also been obtained on film unexposed by a camera.

A recent important development of spiritualism has been in the direction of spirit healing. Unorthodox healings are well known to have occurred in a variety of sacred places throughout the world, such as Lourdes, in France. Sacred rites are alleged to have produced remarkable healings. It is thought by the medical profession that such spontaneous or dramatic healings are the result of the normal process of mental suggestion working under favorable conditions. But it is also possible that there is genuine power to heal, and that this power is manifested through mediums who are the agents of spirit doctors. These are people who were, in fact, physicians when they were on the earth plane. Having had that connection with medicine on the earth plane, in spirit they also bring knowledge of healing from the vast store of human experience.

There is a clear difference between a psychic and a medium. All mediums are psychic, but not all psychics are mediums. Mediums acknowledge that they receive information from a teacher or a guide in the

spirit world. Impressions are received clairvoyantly.

Spiritualist sessions or meetings usually take place in the presence of a medium, someone acting as an intermediary with the spirit world. Although most mediums seem to be women, indeed the movement of spiritualism was begun in this country by two women as noted previously, there have been some highly gifted mediums who were men.

The séance or a circle at which the mediumship phenomena occurs is often held in darkness or reduced light, but occasionally in full daylight. There may be more than one person acting as the medium, although the traditional séance has been focused on a principal medium to whom questions are directed and through whom answers or messages are given. It is not unusual for the medium to be in a trance without memory of what has been said, but some work in the conscious state.

As would be expected, evidential information is the hallmark of any connection between the living and those who are in spirit. Two types of evidence test the communications. First there is the evidence of recognition when the medium describes physical attributes (character, manners of speech, identifying scars, physical descriptions of rooms, houses or geographical locations), of the communicating spirit. Second, there is information known only by the person in spirit (deceased). Such information is looked for and appreciated by the medium, as it reinforces the sense of connectedness with the spirit, and adds to the ever-increasing body of evidential material that solidifies the "faith". For, as in all spiritual endeavors, doubt is an ever present liability. No matter how solid the belief, conformation of it is a gift.

Raymond G. Berube - Nancy Jane Isaacson

CHAPTER SEVEN
Interviews of Circle Participants

Interview with Lisa

This interview was done with a young woman, Lisa, who had been a part of Nancy's circles for some time. From the start I have been impressed with her ability to go rapidly from one member to the next, with several pieces of information for each. She seems very connected. It was, therefore, interesting to me in the course of this interview, to hear Lisa express doubt and underestimate herself.

Lisa first came to Nancy's circle as a referral through someone she met at a Dover, New Hampshire group, years ago. It was the result of networking, something Lisa describes as very important in Spiritualism. It is the principle means by which people find circles to join, and are informed of new groups, churches, and events.

Having sought out the Dover group because of a compelling need to "seek her spiritual path", she was then advised to join Nancy's circles. Lisa explained that her quest stemmed from having experienced emotional upheavals, having been suicidal as a young girl.

"Ray, I had a near-death experience when I was fifteen, as a result of alcohol poisoning. I was suicidal. I was in a coma for almost eighteen hours. When I woke up from that I knew that something had changed in my life. Something had happened; a significant experience, spiritually, but I didn't know what. So I started to read a lot of psychology books, and went to college and got a degree in psychology. I wanted to try and get into a healing process so I could then be able to help others.

"I found a support group, and through networking, found a meditation group, then went to Nancy's circle. I didn't know much about

81

guides, except that I knew I had my own personal guidance, and that there was something more than met the eye.

"About a month into it, I got a very interesting message, and Nancy brought it. She got the name 'Whitney,' who is my great Aunt, and she is in spirit…, her name is Emily Whitney. She died when she was ninety-two, and she was the only relative I knew that was in spirit. Nancy described her, described her character, where she lived, and what it looked like around where she lived. She gave me a message of encouragement.

"It was very evidential, and made me feel like there was definitely something there."

I asked Lisa if she had ever doubted, before. Had she ever been unsure of the possibility of actually connecting with Spirit?"

"I don't know if I was really doubtful, but I think it helped to have confirmation. I was open to it. I already believed in a higher power. The very first time I came to a circle, I felt fear. I was fearing that I was doing something evil, but after I came a couple of weeks, I was fine."

Knowing that this concern is one that many people have, and a belief that many people hold, I was curious as to how Lisa might assure someone who might offer this argument against practicing Spiritualism.

"Do you find a lot of people have that same concern?" I asked. "What do you tell people when they say they fear messing with the devil, or with strange powers? How do you alleviate their fears?"

"That's a hard one. I usually don't go around telling people what I'm doing, so I haven't been criticized that way. But, I would explain that there is a circle available that helps get you in touch with your higher self, and your spiritual development, and developing your own intuition; getting in touch with your higher guidance…., and say that it's connected with healing and with the more intuitive side of yourself."

"And what do you tell someone who says that you're still messing with spirits; you're connected with evil", I pressed. "Lisa, when you go into a circle, how do you prevent or avoid this possibility of evil"?

Lisa laughed. Obviously it was a question that had arisen, or that she had been asked before.

"What Nancy did that helped that whole situation, is she started with a prayer and did meditation with the image of a while light, and incorporated it into Christian beliefs of white Christ-light, God, protection; that only the highest and the best come to us. So that helped me feel real comfortable right away. One of the other most important aspects of the circle is the nurturing that goes on between members, especially in Nancy's circles. I've been to a lot of different circles, and they don't all have that. The caring that goes on between the members…, it comes out in the messages. You're trying to help each other…, and you're trying to develop yourself spiritually. So you're doing two things at once. After a while you start feeling safe when you get to know people. Feels like a support group. You have common friends, and it makes it a community. The circle fills a need and you don't have to do the spiritual path, yourself, you can work on it with others."

I explained that one of the purposes of the book was going to help people seek out or organize home circles.

"With Nancy's circles, she adds touches like for holidays, we would try to do things around a theme. Her own caring and concern; calling one another to make sure everything is alright. And her encouragement, when you're learning! If you start to take risks by giving out messages, she gives you a lot of support so you don't feel alone and being laughed at."

Lisa had impressed me from the beginning, when I had started attending Nancy's circles in the summer of 1992. She seemed extraordinarily tuned in, and would deliver rapid-fire messages for several people, one after the other. I mentioned this, and that I thought she had been practicing spiritualism for a long time, and not just for four years. I asked her to what she attributed her skill?

"I didn't see myself that way at all. I still doubt myself a lot. It's my biggest block, right now. I doubt that I'm bringing in information that is accurate enough. I feel that sometimes I …, I'm worried and I want to know for sure that it's coming from spirit, and not from me. That's a big one. I think, talking about pivotal points, one for me was a couple years ago. One summer, we stated having circles, and we took turns having them at each other's houses. We had it at Betty's and Nancy used the technique she called *Going Solo*. You take the minutes and have the floor for that amount of time, with no one else talking. You give out what you get, right on the spot, and for me it was a pivotal point because when I did that I realized I had the floor. Spirit filled the time with messages. I got more confident because I got more accurate. I gave Nancy some real accurate information, and got my confidence."

This particular situation of having time solely allotted to one person, with silence and no distractions, seems an important element in being able to connect with Spirit. This seems especially true for beginners. It was for me. I said little during my first two months of attendance. This was because I felt unable to receive, as my concentration seemed too focused on the other messages being given out around me. It was not until Nancy introduced a technique for receiving impressions called "billet reading", that I really found my skill and felt confident. The term "billet reading" is explained elsewhere in this text. So when Lisa mentioned her own confidence having been nurtured as a result of "going solo", I fully understood.

"Having some time, and being given the freedom of having quiet time makes the difference. Taking turns is also important. You don't have to worry about waiting for an opening or interrupting someone else's message. It makes the dynamics of the group better.

Lisa continued. "The most important/critical message I've brought, is one to Donna about her Uncle George. She was very close to him, and that brought her to tears. I also brought to someone who works in a hospice, someone who had died of AIDS, and that was meaningful. I've done that a few times; brought people who died of AIDS, younger people, and I get tuned into therm. I think messages regarding people's states of emotional being, their past, future, and present state of consciousness are important; letting them get through emotional blocks and resolving them. Sometimes people have been brought to tears when I've mentioned things they might do to unblock.

"This has all been a gradual process for me. But when I was a child I always had a connection with my guides but didn't realize that that's what people called it. I had guidance and knew I did. I was confident about that, then. So this was just a perfectly natural thing to get into. It's no different from what I've been doing in my life, and that's why I got into psychology. I'd always been reading people. Focusing in on it, I've been able to integrate it into my life and into my work. I teach in industry, doing training programs, and work with people. People have always been drawn to me. So when they come to me with a problem or an issue, I try to use that guidance to give them help.

"I don't make an issue of spiritualism. I just help as though it came from me. I don't blow people away or call it anything. I find much of what I decide or what I advice, has resulted from my guides. People have come up to me and asked how I knew something in particular, how I had a certain piece of information, and I laughed. They are often perplexed as to how I know little things. I've joked and told them I'm psychic, but they don't really know that I'm doing this. I put a lot of time into study, reading a lot of books on channeling, on spiritualism and psychology."

I then asked Lisa to recommend some books she had found helpful, for enlightenment and the expansion of her awareness and abilities.

"Anything by *White Eagle*, White Eagle is a high teacher and author. There's The Quiet Mind, a book about meditation. Those books are written through a channel. Most of what is in those books is the principle of 'love-thy-neighbor'.

"Meditation is important. I probably don't do it enough. Having awareness throughout the day, being aware of your guide and acknowledging their presence, is something they want you to do. I've been told that by my guides, recently. Acknowledging their information seems to make their connection stronger.

"I think I could will this awareness even more than I do. It seems to come spontaneously with me. I'd like to will it more. Some people are harder to tune into than others. You can have on-times and off-times, depending on your condition and that of the event.

"It's important for a leader of a circle to encourage someone who has developed, to move out and start their own circle. Nancy has done that. Now, I've started my own circle and it just grows. I've added some other dimensions, like the laying-on of hands. You can make it individualistic. The leader can make a circle different, and it's important for a leader of a circle not to take over or be dominant; not to feel threatened when someone in a circle has developed to his or her own level. People should be encouraged to grow and move on. Nancy is not egotistical, and she has been able to do that. That's why her circles have been successful; she doesn't have that negativity, and a lot of people do! They have trouble with competition; with people in their circles who may be as good as, or better than they. It's all about growth and letting go. Nancy can do that!"

Interview with Carol

Carol is a former teacher. She travels about, working with school-age children, introducing them to the concept of circles used in the Native American cultures. I asked Carol, as I had asked Lisa, to relate pivotal experiences or events of circles that had been important to her. Carol started with the same time-period related by Lisa, which began four years ago. She said that at the end of the summer meditation class they were looking for something to do to bring them further along the path of spiritual development.

"Bob was part of Nancy's Monday night circle at the time. He suggested that we come and join that. So we did and it was only about six months later that we decided to get involved with the Spiritualist Church. The thing that I remember was the first night of being at Nancy's circle. I was scared to death! It wasn't being scared of spirits but of someone or something coming through that would reveal all the horrible things I had done during my whole life!"

She laughed as she said this, understanding now that this kind of information which would embarrass someone is not likely to be given or disclosed.

"Has that ever happened," I asked, wondering if she had once had a bad experience.

"No, it has never happened. But I was so afraid that first night that it would. I've never heard it happen to anyone, to the best of my knowledge. You don't have to worry about the bad things…, your secrets are safe.

"The second or third time I came to the circle, I had a great aunt who was so fun-loving, and she came to the circle that night, and you could feel her energy during the whole thing…, we laughed! Everything was funny. She was kind of whizzing around the whole place; I didn't see her, but other people could sense and feel her energy. That was a particular experience that was important to me…, an evidential one. A pivotal experience…, I don't know…, I was born and raised in the Catholic Church so spirits were always a kind of a part of my life. My grandparents died when I was a teenager, so I always talked to them, and I knew they were around, so I don't know that I needed a pivotal experience to convince me that there were spirits…, I always knew that!"

Knowing how the Catholic Church appears to frown on Spiritualism and those activities related to it, I wondered how Carol qualified her interest.

"What would you tell a Catholic who would say to you that you were doing dangerous stuff?"

"See, it's trying to convince them of stuff they already know! They know…, they believe in what they call *communion of saints*, that you do go to heaven, and that you don't end as soon as you die. We've been born and brought up on that…, so why not allow these people to be a part of your life even when they go over to Spirit? My Dad died sometime in that first year we were coming, and for the first year after he died, he came to the circle every week. He was here every week with some sort of message or other, and it was only after about a year that we started seeing that he was coming less and less."

"Why was that?" I asked.

"He told me that he was getting more and more involved in the work he was doing. Now he very rarely comes, but he comes to me in moments that I really need him, but seldom to the circle. The same thing happened to my sister. She died about a year ago, and she came fairly frequently. But she's come less and less. It seems that within that first year of when they pass over, that's when they come. But once they know we'll do alright without them, then they get involved in whatever work they do in Spirit…, they go off and do what they have to do."

"What do you feel is important and necessary for you to be

comfortable in the circle?"

"I think it's to be able to trust the people you're with. That whether you get a message or not, it's okay."

This was a point that had bothered me when I had first started attending; the feeling of being useless if you are not able to give out messages. I asked Carol to expound on it.

"I was frustrated, sitting in a circle for about two years with never getting a message. I had to figure out my way of connecting with Spirit and Spirit connecting with me. I have a great difficulty getting messages from what I call *the grand void*, where there's nothing to focus on and you're just sitting there waiting for Spirit to contact you or trying to be in touch with a person..., I can't do that; I should say that it's hard for me to do that! I, however, had great success when we tried different things, and one person in the group would pose a question and we would all focus on that question and try to get an answer..., I could do that. I know astrology, tarot, numerology. I know all those different hands-on things. The way Spirit communicates with me now is, they give me a message, they might show me a particular tarot card or a zodiacal sign to tell me about a planet, or bring an animal or Native American stuff that I'm into..., and focus in on that. Then I can bring in a message. What I seem to be better at doing is interpreting other people's messages. They will say they see this, the other thing, and I can say that these things mean whatever my skill interprets the message to mean.

"The other night, Lisa got a message about wearing a beautiful earring. She didn't know what it meant, but it was immediately clear to me that it meant that she was going to get a clairaudient message, that she was going to be able to hear better. That's what I want to make clear to people; that we don't all do mediumship in the same way..., that we all don't see messages in the same way. When I say 'see' something, it's most always that I sense something."

"Carol, you seem to connect with symbols. Symbols seem to work for you, and intuition. When some people in the group actually hear, and others like Stanley, see spirits right in the room..., you seem to find symbols

and intuition to be your methods."

"I can't do that! But if I see something connected with somebody..., if I see a fox, I know that in the Native American tradition the fox is talking about camouflage, and I would say to that person that they are probably out there too much, or are seen too much..., and perhaps they need to hold back and be more hidden..., or maybe they are too hidden and need to come out more. If I see a coyote, I know they're looking for some kind of foolishness; some kind of lesson that works on by trickery or something like that.

I mostly *sense*. Once in a while I may see an actual picture."

I asked Carol to speak about her guides, and her awareness of them.

"I know that I have guides that have been brought to me for a number of reasons. I have a guide named Long Bow. He is one who works with people when they are doing a creative project, a craft-kind of thing. Just recently Seven Bows, a guide who is very high up, brought me Many Feathers, another Indian guide. He's the one I'm probably closest to right now. When I go into a classroom to work with kids, I open my mouth and he's there. And everything I say is guided by him. He's so much fun to watch. It's just amazing. Just before Christmas I did a series of five workshops in a school. It was around the holiday and the kids were off the wall. The teacher called me up the day before, unsure whether I should do the workshop. I said we would try and see what would happen. If I saw that the kids were not responding, I would pull back! Well I walked in there, and the kids were like angels..., they ate it up. One of the kids approached me after, and said 'you really love what you're doing, don't you!' I admitted it. They knew there was something there."

Carol continued to describe her work with children in the classroom, looking at the concept of how the "circle" was used by Native Americans, interwoven with their beliefs in nature, and how the tribes used the circle to form a governmental structure. She seemed fully committed to this work, and was especially excited with the interest being expressed by children with whom she came into contact.

"That's where I feel my mediumship is going; that's what is most fun and most comfortable, for me. Going into the church and standing on the

podium giving messages is foreign. I can't even begin to imagine that. That whole Native American concept of the circle is what I'm trying to teach.

YOU, THE MEDIUM

I've been a part of so many different types of circles, it's almost hard for me to restrict myself to the spiritualist kind of circle we have here. Almost all the work I do with teachers, in the last four years, has been done in circles. And they are spiritualist circles, but of a different nature. They're all basically getting at the same thing; the safety of a circle, and the power of the circle, the power of knowing that everybody in the circle brings some talent to it. The healing that I have seen going on in circles, and not just spiritualist circles, allows people to express whatever needs to be expressed. There's a healing that goes on, without anyone realizing it."

Interview with Cathy

Cathy has met with our circle, and was the medium through which the historical figure of Antinoos made contact in November of 1993. Since then she has brought him to the group a second time. Cathy appears to have the potential for trance mediumship, and we have been meeting for this specific purpose. She is a wife, mother, and social worker. We have been impressed with her balance and ethical nature, and I was sure she could contribute valuable information to these interviews.

"Cathy, this interview is essentially having to do with home circles, and specifically with Nancy's circles and how those have come about; how they have influenced you. Why do you feel home circles are important to you, since you were at the first circle Nancy held, ten years ago?"

"I think circles give people the opportunity to learn and to test Spirit, with their friends and family. I think that when home circles started, it started with families. They had family members coming into it, also close friends. I think the closeness and safety of a home circle is very important. In a home circle, you build up a trust much easier because it's small. I think you get more. The energy can be built faster. And the results are more effective."

I wondered how she felt about the place-of-meeting for circles. Did she feel more inclined to meet at other favored places outside the home?

"Do you think there is an advantage of meeting in people's houses

instead of church-halls, book stores, or those kinds of places?"

Cathy seemed sure and was quick to respond. "The advantage of having meetings in the home is that you can have a room specifically for the purpose of a circle, and you can keep it more-or-less clean from negative thoughts, and the vibration can be built and maintained with soft music, plants, and flowers. If it's a place that was used specifically to do Spirit work, then people wouldn't be arguing in there, and there would be no negative talk. So in that respect, it's better."

"So you're suggesting that there be a room that's isolated, devoted to just doing circles. That's not an easy thing to do!" I was wondering just how many of us had that much living space these days that allowed for a room to be used for just one purpose.

Cathy continued by describing the difference between the space in a church, and one in the home.

"There's a different vibration in a church because it is a sacred place, so you get the energy of the church, but it's not as pure as having a room specifically for a circle"

I wondered what advise she might offer someone who would be thinking of getting involved in home circles. "What would you tell someone who may have heard you talking about the things you do, and how to check it out?"

"When new people come into the church, I always tell them that if they're wanting to develop, they don't necessarily have to go to a church class, that they should make sure that wherever they go, that the person leading the group always protects them, that they feel safe and listen to be aware that there is no negativity or condemnation being professed in the circle. I always tell them to be aware of a reverence to the circle."

"What do you think might be some red-flags, indicators, that a circle might not be being conducted properly?"

"I would feel cautious of a circle where the people running the circle are trying to control or conduct other people's lives. When Spirit comes through, it comes through as a guiding force, not as an end-all. Anyone that comes through, that says you must do this, you must quit your job, or anything else with that degree of enforcement..., I would question the

accuracy of the information that's coming through."

There are times when messages seem to come through as dogmatic, and this emphasis is most likely the result of the medium's interpretation. I thought this warning a good one! Cathy went on to explain.

"You always need to listen to the quality and intent of the message. It's not so important to know who the message is from, but the message should be spiritual and uplifting, it should guide you into doing something, guide you into making your own choice and not saying that this is the way it is or has to be. Spirit's knowledge is just as limited by how much they've grown as we are, here."

Did she find a need to be cautious about advice received from spirit, I wondered. "Is it a mistake that a lot of people make in assuming that all you hear from spirit must be the truth? Couldn't spirits have misapprehensions, and be wrong?"

"Absolutely! There isn't a medium on the face of the earth that can be one hundred percent right. For one thing, the spirits themselves can have limited knowledge. Secondly, you're at the mercy of the medium who's interpreting what they are being given. People feel, hear, and sense. You might be given the image of a cake with six candles on it, and may give out the message that the spirit is trying to communicate with someone about to have a sixth birthday, and it could actually have something to do with another event such as an anniversary. It would be better for me as the medium interpreting the symbol, to state that the cake represents a six-year event. Then, whoever could connect with the sixth birthday or anniversary could respond with the *appropriate* identification.

"Many people just starting out have a tendency to get in the way of the message. You can tell if they're getting in the way and giving you information about a problem that they have an issue with; something that they should talk to you about instead of presenting under the pretense of spirit; saying that 'Spirit says you should do this, or that…'. I see it happen a lot. They take the opportunity to tell you what *they* want to say, and present it as though Spirit were advising it. So you need to pay attention to the caliber and integrity of the people who act as mediums. And the point should be that the message is helpful to you!"

"Does an event come to mind of a consequential message you received while attending circle, that made a significant change in your life," I asked.

"Yes, one of the most evidential messages I've ever gotten was one given just after a church service. I had gotten up for a healing and the girl that did the healing came up to me and said that there was a spirit that just would not go away, and that she had to give me a message. She just kept saying to me 'I have your father here with me' I said this was impossible because my Dad was still on the earth plane and that unless something had just happened, he was still here.

"She said that she needed to describe this man and described an older gentleman, big in the body, and had grayish shoulder-length hair and that she kept hearing the word "father". She said that his words were to the effect that he hated and was sorry to leave me alone, that he was really sorry!

"I said that I would take the message, and would see what happened with it. I didn't get upset because I did not sense that my Dad had died or anything. Next morning around six o'clock I got a call from the adopted daughter of the president of the board of our agency. This woman said that her step-father had died of a stroke. We were in the middle of a court case requiring much of his attention, and this was shifted onto my shoulders. He came through to me to say he was sorry he was leaving me alone.

"When it occurred to me who the lady at church had been referring to, I realized that her physical description had fit this man perfectly. And the "father" terminology was because he was a minister. He remained in a coma, and I went up to spend time with him and told him that it was alright to leave me alone..., I had the lawyer and it would be okay. I had the members of his family tell him the same thing..., trying to have him understand that he could allow himself to pass, that he was not deserting anyone and that we would be able to get along with our lawyer. The man in coma died the next day."

"What effect did this incident have on you? Did it confirm for the first time, or was it a re-confirmation of the existence and presence of sprits?" I asked.

Cathy smiled. "It simply reconfirmed and just made it clear..., brought it home that there is this reality. I've always had the knowledge that there was someone guiding me, and I always referred to it as my Guardian Angel. I've always known that I was protected and that someone was watching over me just from the events that have happened in my life. I have a tremendous trust in my guiding spirit and even when I don't think I know something, I behave as though I know everything. When I'm doing something, I know what I have to know. I just allow it to flow, and I realize that whatever it is, it's always there when I need it. I'm a social worker and that's how I do my counseling. I've always been able to help people make a transition or to help and comfort families at the time of death.

"Way back in my early twenties when I was newly married, at night I would wake up and there would be a man at the foot of my bed. And I would scream and wake my husband. This man would be standing there, wearing a black cape and a top-hat, and it would scare me. This happened every night. It got to a point that my husband would get really upset, and he wanted to get me checked out, and then it stopped."

"Did you ever find out who it was?"

"It's funny, when I would describe what he looked like, I would say that he looked like a door-man. And that's who he was, my Gate Keeper, the doorman, the Spirit responsible for controlling those spirits who communicate with you. And now that I want him to come back, he's never appeared to me again."

"How long have you been involved in home circles?" I knew Cathy was not new to Spiritualism.

"Since the early seventies, maybe late sixties."

"Did you start with Nancy's circles?"

"No. We had a circle in Gloucester with some friends and myself. Then I went to the Spiritualist Church in Hampton, and then I went up to Nancy's circle."

"In terms of how she conducts her circle, do you see her doing things very differently? How does she conduct them that seems to make them so good?"

"Well, I think one of the things the other circles did was try a lot of

things that we'd read about. With Nancy, we knew that she had been born into Spiritualism and knew that there was a proper way to conduct a circle. I think because she starts off with a prayer and protection and a song, that she raises the vibration. And she has the ability to tune in and know what's happening within a circle, and therefore is helpful in guiding someone who is developing and brings him along. She makes you feel safe, knowing that there is someone there to help. She'll guide you, asking whether you feel something or sense something. That helps. It plays an important role."

Given all that Cathy said, I wondered just how much she had been affected by her experiences.

"How have you been changed, because of circles?"

"I certainly have become more aware of what has

been going on around me. There have also been a lot or personal developments, such as patience and tolerance, accepting people for who they are! It has helped me to develop not only personally, but also intuitively in my work…, to be able to hear better, to be there with my patients."

"How about your inside spirituality…, your own spiritual growth?"

"Well, that is tough to talk about because I have some strong feelings about the word *spiritual.* There are so many people that say that they are spiritual."

I could tell that she had some strong opinions about how the word and the concept of spirituality are misused. She continued, with caution.

"So many say, 'I'm a spiritual person.' But what makes you a spiritual person? You go to church every Sunday and you smile…, and then you see a black person and you spit at them, maybe not literally, but the attitude really belies the prejudice and denies the act of spirituality."

I understood perfectly what she meant, and responded.

"To me, the spiritual person is the one who is driving down the street, sees a driver waiting to turn into the traffic from a side street with a line of cars passing without anyone giving that person a break, and slows down to allow them in. The spiritual person is the one who allows other people to be who they must be without passing judgment; who does not give lip-service to human values, but lives them!"

Cathy concurred. "To me, being spiritual is treating others as you want to be treated. People think they are spiritual because they don't swear. I swear a lot, but I can be just as spiritual."

"I'm going to put you on the spot with this next question, Cathy. It's a question I always have, and did have some weeks ago when I attended a circle held by Bill Rowan (an Australian medium touring the U.S.). Bill channeled information, and the topic was on home circles. He stated that Spiritualism began as hone circles, and this is where it needed to return. The entity that Bill brought stated that at first, home circles organized into networks, and networks formed groups that called themselves churches, and these churches set up rules, laws, regulations, setting into place controls. The essence of home circles became lost in the morass of organizations! The message given was that we need to get back to the simplicity of home circles.

"I know that you belong to a church, and you believe very strongly in home circles. Is there a dichotomy, for you?"

Cathy laughed. "A few years ago I upset the pastor of my church because she said I needed to go to church. I told her that I did not need the church, but the church *needs* me. I take the church with me wherever I go…, I'm my own church!"

"That's a tough one for Catholics to handle," I said.

"In a recent reading, the medium brought me my dad. The discussion was about churches and Catholicism. Although my dad was a Catholic, the religion did not meet all his needs. Dad spoke through the medium with the message that the street where he lived was his church. For him, religion was not so much a meeting place as it was a way of life. That was something that was really ingrained in me because I grew up in the North End (Boston), and he was very well known simply because if you needed something and my father knew you needed it, he would just give it to you!

"I like to go to church because it's where I meet people of like mind. But it's not an absolute need. I was taught that we are created in the image of God. We are the temples of the spirit."

Here, the irony of organized religion and independent spirituality was obvious.

"Organized religion came in, and men began to create laws to control

the masses and they put the fear of God in you. The *fear* of God instead of the *love* of God! It should be the love and the *joy* of God."

"Just one more question," I pressed. Cathy had been patient, but looked tired.

"What is it that you do on a daily basis to prepare yourself or set yourself up for your communications to happen. How do you sense your guides or spirits?"

"When my alarm goes off at a quarter to six, I shut it off and stay in bed. For the next fifteen minutes I talk to God. I tell him about what I expect to face during the day, and ask for help. I ask him to help me keep me aware of his presence, and knowing that he's there, all I have to do is ask for his help. Sometimes I drift off, but I always wake up at six, without the alarm. That's probably all I do on a daily basis, as far as meditation is concerned. You know..., I feel plugged in, but not plugged in to a spirit connection. Because of the social work that I do, I would never tell someone that one of their dead relatives was present, however, I say the right thing to them. Someone in spirit is there helping me tell that person what they need, but I don't tell the patient or client that.

"That's where my mediumship link is very strong, in my daily work! I use my mediumship differently. I know I can make connections when I sit in circle, but I don't do that on a daily basis. My strongest mediumship is when I'm working, on a day-to-day basis. I don't know why I say most of what I say to anybody. Sometimes a question just triggers an answer. It's almost as though that's what makes me connect."

Being curious about Cathy's feelings about our book writing project, I asked why she thought anyone would want to buy our book on home circles.

"I think this book will help everybody realize that we're all born with this ability in that we all need to make our own connections. It's a birthright that we have. It's part of us, and something that lies dormant within us. This book will show how others have done it and give others inspiration to take the step and make the effort."

Interview with Richard

I first met Richard when I began attending Nancy's home circles in the summer of 1992. Richard works with Special Needs young people, and is also an actor. He is a very capable and efficient medium who has the amazing ability to deliver messages in a rapid-fire way, going from one person to the other with few pauses. Where many mediums speak slowly and often spend moments in silence, tuned to the reception of the messages, Richard seems to be flooded with information and is able to deliver almost continuously.

Given his proficiency, I wondered how long Richard had been psychic.

"What were some of your earliest memories of psychic abilities?"

"I remember when I was young, about five or six years old, my grandmother, who was also psychic, supported me in this. I would have a lot of imaginary friends which I saw, that we would have for dinner and she would set a place for them and she would see them. My father was not supportive of it, and my mother was not supportive either.

"I remember when I was young and when there were missing things around the house, I would tell them where they were and would get punished for it because they thought I had hidden them on purpose."

"You were that accurate that they believed you responsible?"

"I was extremely accurate. I remember a time, about five or six, when the family went on a trip to the mountains. I warned my father before we set off that he needed to bring extra gas because we would run out. He said he would be alright because he had filled the tank. Well, about thirty minutes after we left, sure enough, the car ran out of gas. Apparently there had been a gas leak or something wrong with the gauge. Anyway, we did run out of gas and we were stuck!

"From earliest times I would get an impression, like a feeling that something was going to happen…, that it had already happened…, and I didn't have any words for it but I knew these things, and I knew I was right!"

"How old were you then?"

"About five or six. When I was in my teenage years, my impressions

came in my dreams. I had a lot of dreams about people and events that I didn't know. This was quite disconcerting to me so I pushed it aside for a period of time.

"Another thing that I should mention is that when I was about two years old, I died for about six or seven minutes. This is on record at the Boston Children's Hospital. I was rushed to the hospital after having chocked on popcorn. They actually pulled the sheet over my head after taking me off the stuff that had been helping me to breathe, when they were convinced I had died. They said that I was gone! Now I don't recall seeing the light that people with near-death experiences talk about, but I did see a lady who pushed me back. It wasn't until some years later while looking at photographs, that I saw her and said I knew the lady. My mother informed me that this was impossible because it was my grandmother on my father's side, who had died before I was born.

"For a long time I pushed all this back, and tried repressing these feelings and sensations, especially in high school and my teenage years. I really didn't do much with it. Later a friend of mine suggested that we attend a psychic church. When I walked in and the medium said to me, 'you are an extremely strong psychic; you have lots of people around you.' I didn't know what she meant. I started to investigate this more and went to a circle at one time where there was one medium that helped me to develop. I really didn't know what it was, but I knew I had hunches, ideas that things were going to happen but I never had a label for it."

If Richard had had this gift from an early age, I wondered what kind of influence or guidance he had received from his family.

"Did your parents recognize this gift, when you were a child? Did they do anything to foster it?"

"My parents did not foster anything. My mother had psychic ability. She understood this, but never wanted to develop it. I think it was something that she was very nervous about. She is in spirit, now. My grandmother was a very accurate psychic, and had very strong ideas about it. But my mother said it was because she was "crazy", and made it look like she never took her very seriously. I used to enjoy her, but she died before I was a teenager.

"It was kind of fun for me when I was younger because I never thought of it as being very important to me. I knew I had premonitions and ideas that things were going to happen, and this would scare the heck out of my mother. The thing that scared her most was when I predicted when her uncle was going to die. I sensed that he was going to go in spirit because one of my little friends told me that they had a place for him, that they were preparing it for him; that he was going to pass. When I had gone to the hospital, my little friend said "they have place for that guy!" (Here, Richard is referring to the childhood playmates which only he and his grandmother could see.) So when I told my mother, she didn't think much about it until when he passed. Then she told me that I couldn't do this stuff anymore because it wasn't good for me. She discouraged it.

"Was this because of any certain religious beliefs." I asked.

"Yes, my mother raised me as a Catholic and I went to parochial school for about three or four years. It was something that was not encouraged in the church. But if you look in the Bible, you'll find it throughout. All the prophets had visions! I had a friend who was a Seventh Day Adventist, and they were very strongly against that stuff. When I went to one youth group, we read about Jacob having dreams and I said that I also had those experiences. My friend told me that my dreams were of the devil."

This statement of Richard's pointed to an irony so prevalent in Christian religious beliefs.

"So, *seeing* was okay for the saints and prophets,
but not for common man!"

"Exactly! The common man could not do this. But I always felt that my ability was something God-given. People have different philosophies about who can do this and who can't. I think that most people have the ability to do this, but that some have it stronger. Everybody can draw to some extent, but some have artistic ability that seems to be innate, it's part of them, a natural ability!"

"Has this ever frightened you?"

"I think it frightened me during my adolescent years. I would have terrible dreams of people. Floods and hurricanes, and I knew that these

were about people, but I really didn't know what to do with it. When I saw my first apparition it was so clear to me that it was like a person. But then I realized later that it was a spirit, and that was frightening, my very first visitation. This was something that was controlled. I had gone to a workshop on how to go about the physical materialization of people. I remember asking my spiritual guide to visit me, and he did. I saw him. It was definitely a person in a long, black overcoat and a hat of the colonial period, and he was there about nine or ten feet away! I later came to know him as Paul. He comes to me once in a while. I have about six guides around me that come when they're interested. I have a guide interested in the theatre, who makes his presence known when I'm involved in a production. I can feel him around me."

"What made you get involved in circles?" not all mediums work through the format of home circles. Many are connected with Spiritualist churches, and others prefer to be independent.

"I think the more you use this ability, because it's a lot like the exercising of any other skill or talent, the more practice you get, the stronger it gets. Nancy's was one of the first formal circles I ever attended. I was nervous for the first time because I thought it was going to be a challenge.

"I had gone to a larger circle once before, with a lot of budding mediums and I didn't say anything even though I had a lot of messages for people, because I was so unsure and worried that I might be wrong. You know, I was worrying that if I said something wrong I might look or feel foolish. When I was first starting out, a lot of my information was symbolic. Many times symbols mean something to the recipient, and not to the medium. If I see lemons or bananas all around you, these things might mean something to you but not to me. It's funny but these messages might be simple things your guides give you to prove they are there. The message of lemons might go to someone who responds by saying 'yes, I did buy lemons this afternoon…,' or, 'I was just thinking of getting lemons to help treat my cold!'

"As I was saying, Nancy had asked me to come to this small circle. The feeling around it was wonderful because the other people were all supportive, wishing everyone to be successful. This is the wonderful thing

about those circles…, even when the participants (sitters) are not sure at the moment of what you're bringing them, they say that they will accept it. It may come to them later on."

This situation of a message being brought to someone, and it not initially being understood or identified, happens fairly frequently. Often, recognition comes as a later recall of an event. Everything suddenly becomes clear.

Richard continued. "This happened to me once, when a medium said something and said that she didn't know what she was talking about and I didn't either. Then about a week later, all of a sudden I remembered the information and it all became clear. These home circles help people who are just starting out. They are a good support!"

"Richard, what would you tell someone who was just starting out who, like you, might be sitting there getting impressions. How would you urge them to connect?"

"I think you have to tell people to stay with what they are getting. It may not mean anything to you, but the message is not intended for you! It's intended for somebody else.

"I remember last week, when I saw a body of water around a person to whom I was giving a message, and I got an incredible sadness around this body of water. It affected me, and I said to myself that I had to give this out even though it sounded stupid, but she knew exactly what I was talking about. It all clicked, for her. It wasn't intended for me, it was intended for her!

"Then again, you might be sitting with someone and not get anything for that person. I recall a sitting when I was doing psychometry, (this is where a reading is given that relates to an item submitted by the person) and giving a reading around a ring that had been offered, giving out all kinds of information. The person to whom I was giving the message said that nothing related to him. So I said 'Do you own that ring?' He said. 'Oh no, I bought this from someone.' Here, the problem might have been that I was getting impressions of the first owner from the ring and not for the person who was wearing it at the time.

"So, you might be a good channeller for one person but not good for

someone else. This doesn't mean you are a bad medium. There are just good and poor channels."

"What have you gained from attending circles, Richard? What has been your most significant or important experience, while in a home circle?"

"I have gained confidence in my ability to give messages. I get a lot of support. I get a lot of energy, and it follows me through the week. I feel wonderful for days, after I've attended a circle. The energy I get from all the people and spirits there is great.

"My most significant event, well…, I've had a few. I can remember one time when someone brought my uncle. His appearance was described accurately; the pipe that he smoked; the clothing he wore; his personality…, everything was right to the T! This person never met my uncle and there was no way that he could have known this information, yet he was absolutely correct! That's pretty thrilling. It was a nice experience to know that my uncle was nearby. It's wonderful to get the confirmation from people. But you must remember that you are not doing it! I don't think that any good spiritualist or medium can really take the credit for bringing messages through, because it's the guides that are doing it. You must act as a channel. To think that you are doing it by yourself is a mistake. You've got to give your guides credit. I always end with 'I want to leave you with the love and blessing from Spirit.' I think that this is important, to acknowledge the spirits. I want to thank my guides because I know that I couldn't do all this by myself. I know I'm not doing it,

"There's danger, also, you can't put your own stuff in it. A lot of times mediums do that. You may be reading for people you know and there's a tendency to interpret the message and you want to say that thing means this or that. That's the danger. You should just say what you sense, give the message, say what you hear the voice saying, and nothing more. Think of yourself as a big antenna bringing the signal through. The antenna does not speak or think or restate, it just projects what it gets. I just give what I receive."

I wanted Richard to reflect on what he would feel would be the elements of a good circle, and what he would identify as possibly being a

bad circle, and how he would warn newcomers to look for anything that was less than legitimate and honest.

"One warning sign would be if people were charging money for a circle. It's different with a class where someone might be teaching skills development. But at a home circle, someone charging to attend would make me suspicious. I was in a circle once where there was a little cost, but it was going toward the church, and that's fine. People might also contribute a small amount to buy refreshments. But if a leader of a circle says they are going to charge an amount and it's going for their own profit, then that's a warning.

"There's also a danger of having people who are just there to get a message. You've got to have a good blend of energy and that comes from picking and putting together a good group of people. Nancy's circles always seem to work because there's always a nice blend of energy. It is a danger if you have people who are just there for the show.

"A good medium will feel the skepticism if there is any. This can really put a damper on the energy when you have someone attending circle who is skeptical or un-believing, and is just resistant and negative. So, the circle's integrity is maintained by minimizing negative people and negative energy. You don't have to prove your ability to anybody. You don't need to prove mediumship to people. You shouldn't need to have to perform and give out someone's middle name or predict tomorrow's temperature just to prove something. The real proof occurs when SPIRIT chooses. If people want information from you that is not significant, the guides are not going to give it!

"You want people in your circles who are not there with the attitude of 'prove it to me', but who already know the phenomenon exists. You want people who want to give, or receive, or develop their skill and that's a good circle when you have that combination of people."

I wanted Richard to speak to those people who might have interest in home circles, but may not have attended any or who may be anxious about the kind of participations they would bring to one.

"What would you say to someone who comes to a circle with genuine interest but does not seem, for a while anyway, to be getting

anything in the sensing of messages from spirit? What benefit would someone like that bring to a circle, if any?"

"I would say that it takes a while when you're first starting, to begin receiving. Just the fact that they are there and have interest, shows that they want to connect. I'm sure that they will eventually get something. Some people are receptive almost without training, they have a natural gift. But we all have the ability, and with sincerity and persistence, something will begin to happen. It takes practice. The more you sit in a circle, the more you tune yourself , the better you expect to become proficient without practice or training. I think a new person's presence brings energy. If they come every week, they will bring a special energy with them, and that's a terrific contribution to a circle. You know, a car is useless without its battery to start it!

"I can remember one man who waited and waited without getting anything. Finally after weeks, he told me about seeing a bird around me, one swooping into my windshield, and he said 'I'm afraid you're going to hit it.' He was confused by the vision and it didn't mean anything to me at the time. So I said that although I did not understand the message, I would accept it and thanked him. Two days later while I was driving along a country road and looking at the trees near Keen, New Hampshire, I suddenly caught sight of a bird flying directly for my windshield and swerved my car in time to avoid the bird and the ditch I would have likely driven into. That's when I remembered the man's message. As soon as I got home, I phoned him to confirm the event. He was so happy to hear that he had given me a clear message. This seemed to be his starting-point to being able to give messages.

"Once you get your first hit and you get something real definite, the door seems to open. So many people sit there and do get impressions, but wonder if they are correct, or if the thought is really from spirit and not of their own stuff. They just don't give anything out. It takes courage and encouragement. My advice to anyone is, *just say it*!"

I recalled my own ambivalence to speaking out when I first started at Nancy's circle. As described earlier in this book, it wasn't until I took a chance that I began to blossom.

"You have nothing to lose and everything to gain," I said to Richard, "by taking a risk and speaking of what you sense."

Richard agreed. "By giving out what you sense, you benefit yourself by getting information and you also benefit the person for whom the information is intended. When you don't give out a message sometimes, it's almost like having taken the time to buy and wrap a gift for somebody and not giving it. It remains wrapped and unused, unseen. That's how it seems to me that you deprive people of a gift. Messages are gifts to people from those in spirit who know a lot more than we do of what is going on.

"I have been helped and encouraged people I've met in home circles to develop my senses. Sometimes, I'll get odors, but mostly my strong point is that I hear voices and see an image. Sometimes I get sensations. These various ways of receiving, come with development. I'm not very good with names! I've sat in circles where people have given first and last names. I think that Spirit works through you in a way that you will understand and uses your best faculties. My very strong point is that I usually describe the person. I will see people. I can have apparitions appear, and I will describe the person in spirit with great accuracy."

I have been present when Richard has done this and he has amazed me with his accuracy and the proficiency of data he has been able to provide. I wondered if there was a connection with sensing spirit and a person's best receptive skill.

"Do you feel that there is a connection with how a person receives messages from spirit and their learning mode? Some people appear to be visual learners, auditory learners, and others learn best by touching and doing…, tactile learners. Have you found any connection with those?"

"I think so," he said. "I think it does. Such as my own interest being in theater and having done many theatrical things, my imagery is very creative in nature. I feel a lot of things. I feel the emotions. I see the image because it's mostly visual, and sometimes auditory. I think that people like accountants and bookkeepers, detail-oriented people, should pursue the development of their psychic abilities. They could be so accurate because they're so detailed! These are the people who could give names and dates, numbers, and that would be the mode that spirit would use with them. They

would make things very detailed and these detail-type people would be excellent at picking this stuff up. But see, these people are so concrete, and all this sensing from spirit is so abstract, that they can't pull it together. But if they joined a circle and wanted to perceive, they could be very accurate and detailed."

This was an aspect of gathering the correct kind of people for a circle that had not occurred to me. And I found Richard to have struck on an important insight.

"That's interesting. Hopefully anyone in that kind of profession who might be reading this book will be stimulated to have a little more faith in their psychic abilities and realize that they too, have much to learn and contribute.

"Richard, how long have you been doing this? I know that you said since childhood, but I'm talking about home circles."

"About five years."

"How have you found yourself incorporating your psychic abilities on a daily basis?"

"People who know that I am a medium will ask me questions and seek me out. But I'm not really good at getting things for myself. I need to go to a psychic or medium. As a medium, you're a go-between. And it's hard to be a go-between for yourself. That's my philosophy. I talk to psychics who claim to get things for themselves, but I don't do that well. I need to go sit in a circle or be around other mediums to get things for myself. I'm so stubborn that even when I might get a personal message, I might just ignore it and do what I want to do by convincing myself that the sensing was my own "stuff". You don't want to hear things about yourself. So, I don't get a lot of things for me."

"How do you hone your skill, Richard? Is there anything else you do for yourself aside from attending home circles?"

"Yes, I meditate, usually in the morning and evening. And I also go to places that I know my spirit guides enjoy, like the mountains or the sea shore. But meditation is important and I do it in the morning and evening.

"Also, the minute I leave my front door I put a White Light of Protection around me. I do a double charge of that at night before I go to

sleep as well. When you are a magnet to spirits, you want to make sure you get all of the best around you. You don't want evil. I would never do anything like the Ouija Board or tarot cards. I don't believe in crystals…, it's not that I think they're bad, I just don't use them. But I think the other things are harmful! (The reader should know that there are many spiritualists who do not share this opinion) When you're doing things like that, you're fooling with spirits that want to play and you are not going to get the best.

"A lot of times beginning psychics will use playing-cards or will read palms…, I may hold someone's hand while giving a personal reading and look at their palm, but this is more to get the vibration of the person, because I'm not really studying the lines of their palm. This will often be helpful to connect with someone, and as I said, to get the vibration."

Richard's generous responses to my questions mirrored his rapid delivery of information from spirits whenever I have observed him in circle. He is so matter-of-fact about all that he does and of his amazing ability to receive from spirit with a facility I have not often seen, that you come away with the feeling that he sees his gift as something quite common. Richard believes that this ability is in each of us. Developing the skill of spirit communication in a home circle will put you on your path, making **YOU, THE MEDIUM.**

GLOSSARY

APPORT: a physical object appearing spontaneously from the Spirit World

BAND: the "inner band" is a group of spirits who are guides that have assigned roles. They have life-long contact with those they guide. The "outer band" is composed of spirits who guide us intermittently and are attracted to us for specific and sometimes temporary purposes.

BILLET: a note written to someone in spirit from which a medium senses a spirit's response.

CIRCLE: a group of people meeting on a regular basis for spiritual and psychic development.

CHANNEL: a new-age term for medium. As a noun, it means one who is a conduit for spirit messages. As a verb, it means to give a message, usually while in a semi-trance, allowing a spirit to use one's body as a means to speak.

ECTOPLASM: substance drawn from the etheric body of the medium and used by spirit to give form and shape through which spirit manifests.

GUIDE person in Spirit who chooses to dedicate time to advise or influence the physical development of people on the Earth plane.

HEALING: the act of using one's body as a transmitter of healing powers from Spirit.

MEDITATION: an altered state of consciousness which has a point of focus through which people attain

deep relaxation and spiritual growth.

MEDIUM: one who serves as a conduit for the exchange of information between the earth plane and the spirit plane. All mediums are psychic but not all psychics are mediums.

MEDIUMSHIP: the ability, through a connection with Spirit, to use any of many types of mental or physical means to demonstrate the continuity of life.

PARA SENSORY PERCEPTION: the ability to perceive Spirit through all of the senses: seeing, touching, hearing, smelling and including the sixth sense, the psychic "knowing".

PSYCHIC: one who is able to perceive information from the universal consciousness.

PSYCHOMETRY: touching objects and sensing vibrations from them from which messages are received.

"TO SIT" attending a circle or gathering consisting of at least one other person, for the purpose of receiving messages from a person in the spirit world.

SPIRITUALISM: an ancient and modern belief system that teaches personal responsibility. It teaches that man is a soul with a body and that at death, the soul can communicate with those on the earth plane. Communication between the two worlds is possible through people (mediums) who develop their para-sensory perception.

SPIRIT: God, or the collection of spirits who occupy the world of Spirit.

TRANCE: a state of altered consciousness.

TRUMPET: instrument used to amplify a spirit voice, usually performed while in trance, by a medium.

1. Ruth Montgomery tells about Rev. Panton's séance room as one in which she experienced her first séance, in her biography. Ruth Montgomery, Herald of the New Age, with Joanne Garland. On page seventy-two, Ruth tells about visiting Rev. Panton. She heard of him through her sister-in-law, Rhoda Montgomery, who sat with my parents in Rev. Panton's development class.

About The Authors

Raymond G. Berube, M.Ed. is a teacher, author, therapist currently living in Aachen Germany with his partner of 21 years. He has studied hypnosis, NLP, and Stress Management. Raymond has trained with Dr. Milton H Erikson and Dr.Piero Ferrucci of Florence, Italy in 1986 while there doing research for a novel about Emperor Hadrian, on sale with Amazon. He has experienced numerous international cities in his travels and these experiences have come to fruition in the collections of short stories in two volumes, also available at Amazon.com. At present he is a tutor of English to young people and also teaches English as a second language to adults. He has been involved with Spiritualism and mediumship in the past, resulting in two books titled You, The Medium, and Simon Speaks. He has also authored several novels and collections of short stories, all available at a major internet book ordering site.

Nancy Jane Isaacson holds a Bachelor of Science degree summa cum laude, from the University of Vermont where she was initiated into Omicron Nu Honor Society. With a major in Preschool Education, she has taught preschool and early intervention for over twenty years. Nancy is a third generation, life-long Spiritualist. After attending many home circles, she started her own. It began on June 24, 1984 and was open to people wanting to develop mediumship. Being a Spiritualist was not a requirement. At this writing the circle has been meeting regularly for 29 years. On August 4, 1996 Nancy began serving churches in Up State New York ,Massachusetts, New Hampshire, Rhode Island and Maine as a lecturer, Healer, and Message Bearer. She acknowledges that she could not have achieved any of the above without the guidance and love from her spirit guides. She is working on her memoir, "The Making of a Medium." Ray and Nancy met when both worked together as counselors in a group home for people with mental illnesses. He joined her circle and became a great asset within it.
Nancy is the mother of two daughters, four grandchildren, three step grandchildren and six step great grandchildren. The latest joy in her life is starting a circle for psychic children.

"I have had many inspirational teachers in my life, my parents being my first. Now I am passing along what I have learned. I know you will enjoy our book if you want to know what mediumship is and if you want to know how to become one," says Nancy.

www.ingramcontent.com/pod-product-compliance
Lightning Source LLC
Chambersburg PA
CBHW061752020426
42331CB00006B/1440